JANE ASHER'S
PARTY CAKES

THE FUNDAY TIMES

Gerry celebrates
birthday todny

JANE ASHER'S
PARTY CAKES

PELHAM BOOKS

Contents

TO
*Gerald, Katie, Alexander
and my Mother*

Photographs by
BRYAN WHARTON

Illustrations by
GERALD SCARFE

First published in Great Britain by
Pelham Books Ltd
44 Bedford Square
London WC1B 3DU
October 1982
Second impression November 1982

British Library Cataloguing in Publication Data

Asher, Jane
  Party cakes.
  1. Cake
  I. Title
  641.8'653   TX771

ISBN 0-7207-1412-5

Typeset by Rowland Phototypesetting Ltd
Bury St Edmunds, Suffolk

Printed in Great Britain by
Penshurst Press Limited,
Tunbridge Wells

Introduction

When I had been decorating cakes for a few years, I remember my father saying to me that he thought they were getting so good that it was hard to tell them from shop-bought ones. I'm not sure if that was true or whether the cakes were being seen through the rose-tinted spectacles of a loving parent, but in any case it struck me then that if I was going to take the time and trouble to ice a cake it was crazy to have it end up looking as if it had been done impersonally by some professional in a bakery. From then on I resolved to make my cake designs original, unusual, and hopefully relevant to the person for whom they were made.

Any standard cake-icing book will tell you how to produce all the varieties of piping which can give the traditional cake its beauty, and indeed I think it's very useful to have such a book and to practise some of the techniques described. But I hope this book will inspire you to use these techniques to create some new effects – and also to realise that there are many ways of producing a highly competent decoration without having to be technically proficient at all.

I remember a needlework teacher at school trying to impress on me that the stitches that weren't going to show were just as important and had to be just as neat as the ones that were, whereas I tended to go for short cuts and be impatient to create a quick effect. I'm afraid she didn't really manage to convince me, and in my sewing, cooking and cake-decorating I still try to cut corners wherever I can and spend the time on the final obvious details rather than on the unseen work beneath.

For instance, as far as ingredients go there are many ways of saving time and energy without losing any quality – you can spend hours making your own marzipan and fondant: mix royal icing by hand because the books tell you that a mixer will leave too many bubbles, and so on, but I would much rather spend that time in making my design more intricate and highly finished.

My discovery of fondant a few years ago made an enormous difference to my cake making. I think to cover a cake smoothly with royal icing – a very basic step – is one of the most difficult stages of decoration, and one that I never really mastered to my satisfaction. Now that one can just roll out a piece of fondant and slip it over, far more time and energy can be spent on personal touches, and the smooth, ice-rink surfaced royal icing cakes can be left to the

professionals. If I do use royal icing as a base then I cover it with masses of decoration to hide all the bumps and dents.

Most of the cakes have been remade for the book from designs I had done before: a few are new ideas. I started the book when I was about seven months pregnant with my second child, and to get all the cakes made, decorated and photographed at every stage became quite a race against my delivery date. Luckily Alexander arrived a week late, as we were still frantically icing up to the last minute (hence my very swollen hands in some of the detail photographs).

I realised that it would be difficult for me to bake all the cakes in time for me to decorate them, so I enlisted the help of a friend who is an excellent baker. This is another good idea for giving yourself extra time – if you have a friend who enjoys baking then you can make a good team.

I do hope this book will inspire some of you to be adventurous in your cake decorating – I hope it helps to know that of course the ones in the book have been done by a complete amateur, in an ordinary kitchen without any special equipment, and under the same conditions as many housewives: in other words among dogs, cats, children and chaos! I also of course had to clear everything away every evening before I could prepare the supper, and all the normal demands of shopping, cooking and ferrying my daughter to and from school etc. had to continue as usual. Everything in all the cakes is edible, save for the odd cocktail stick or two and a piece of gauze, and we have never cheated in the photographs – I have read stories of how they paint food with varnish and so on for advertisements, but much as this might have been tempting I can assure you all the pictures are completely untouched and of cakes made entirely according to the accompanying description.

I could never have managed to complete all twenty-four in time without help, and I would like to thank my mother who came in and did a lot of tedious clearing up, Mrs Llewellyn for her excellent baking, Shirley Freeman and Flora Casement who became my very efficient assistants for a few weeks, and Bryan Wharton who took time off from his extremely distinguished journalistic career to come and photograph infinitesimal bits of icing.

Finally I must thank my husband and daughter, without whose love and support I would never have attempted or carried out what has been a highly enjoyable project.

Notes on the Recipes

I have divided the cakes into different categories: easy, medium and difficult, but this obviously involved very subjective decisions and shouldn't put you off attempting any of them – you may find certain things more difficult than I did, and vice versa. I have also advised how far ahead to start each cake, but in each case this is the very least time that will be needed as I would recommend on the whole starting as early as possible.

As I wanted these cakes to keep for some time I have used a rich fruit cake mixture in every case, but if you are making one for a children's party then almost certainly they would prefer a different type. Sponge is too light to work with in most cases and could also not be made in advance, but a good chocolate or orange madeira will do very well. You can still use marzipan on these if wished, but it is not essential.

I always use flour instead of icing sugar for rolling out – it keeps things much less sticky, is cheaper and can easily be brushed off.

For sticking you can either use jam, sieved and warmed with a little water, or some royal icing.

Equipment

(Addresses, p.15)

BAKING TINS

All the cakes in this book can be made from these six tins:

a) LOAF-TIN   Must be straight sided.
  20×13×9cm (8″×5″×3½″)
b) ROUND   20cm (8″)
c) ROUND   15cm (6″)
d) SQUARE   23cm (9″)
e) PUDDING BASIN   1 litre (1½pt), ovenproof
f) BAKING TRAY   Mine is 47×35cm (18½″×14″), but smaller will do

a

b

c

d

8

e   f

CAKE BOARDS
The thin ones are cheaper and look neater. They can be ordered by post in any size.

TURNTABLE
Can be a great help but is not essential.

ROLLING-PIN AND BOARD
A good wooden rolling-pin and a large smooth surface for rolling out are essential.

ICING BAGS AND TUBES
I believe professionals twist pieces of greaseproof paper into bag shapes and drop tubes into them, but I find it much easier to use the standard nylon icing bags and the Tala screw fitting and tubes. All the cakes in the book can be made if you have tubes no. 1, 2, 3, 5, 9, 35.

CANDLES
As well as the ordinary birthday candles some of these designs use some very long thin candles that I discovered recently. They come in all different colours and can be useful for all sorts of different ideas.

RULER
Either an icing ruler or just an ordinary wooden one will be useful.

BAKEWELL PAPER
Absolutely essential – used in most of the recipes.

PLASTIC BAGS
Small bags to keep fondant icing in to prevent it drying out.

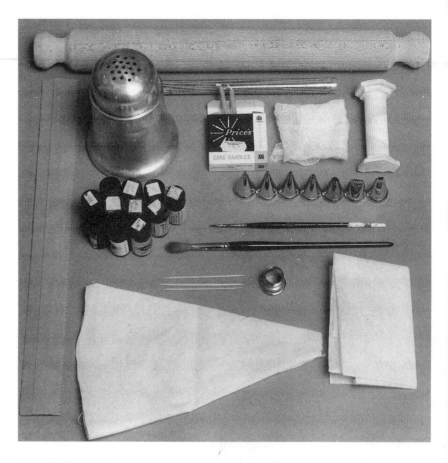

PLASTICINE
Some non-toxic plasticine is sometimes useful for propping things up until they are dry.

PAINT BRUSHES
One fine and one medium will probably be sufficient.

COCKTAIL STICKS
Wooden ones are used in some of the designs for marking fondant and occasionally for propping up.

FLOUR SHAKER
Very useful for dusting the fondant and marzipan while rolling them out.

GAUZE
Used in the baby's cradle. Ordinary gauze from any chemist.

Edible Equipment

RICH FRUIT CAKE

Line cake tin with double thickness of greaseproof paper. Sift the flour with the salt and spices into mixing bowl, then divide this mixture into three portions.

Mix one portion with the fruit and almonds and set aside. Beat the butter until soft, add the lemon rind, sugar and black treacle. Continue beating until the mixture is very soft. Add the eggs, one at a time, beating well between each one, then fold in a second portion of the flour mixture. Next mix in the fruit and flour, then the remaining flour mixture and lastly the brandy or rum.

Turn the mixture into the prepared tin and smooth the top. Dip your fingers in warm water and moisten the surface very slightly (this prevents the cake crust from getting hard during the long cooking). Put the cake in the centre of the pre-heated oven and after one hour reduce the temperature to 160°C/325°F/gas mark 3 and cover the top with double-thick greaseproof paper. Test after 2 hours with a skewer; when done allow to cool in the tin for about 30 minutes, then turn out onto a rack and leave until quite cold.

Wrap in greaseproof paper or foil and store in an airtight container.

MARZIPAN

You can of course make your own, but I prefer to save time and buy it ready-made. Most of the brands are quite acceptable but do give the packet a little squeeze before you buy it – there are a few very unyielding types that I find almost impossible to work with. Sainsbury's own brand is very malleable and also very tasty.

FONDANT

Again, you can make your own by mixing icing sugar with liquid glucose and a little white fat, but I have recently been buying this ready-made also. You can get small quantities now from supermarkets (very useful in emergencies) but generally I do recommend ordering by post. I like Baker Smith's the best. One packet of fondant in the list of ingredients is the equivalent of 500g (1lb). To colour fondant, knead drops of food colouring into the fondant bit by bit until the desired shade is reached. Keep kneading until the colour is even.

INGREDIENTS

(Quantity for 20cm (8") round cake tin)

Try to make at least 2 to 3 weeks ahead.

250g (8oz) plain flour
pinch of salt
½ teaspoon ground cinnamon
1 teaspoon ground nutmeg
1kg (2lb) mixed fruit
125g (4oz) almonds, blanched and shredded
175g (6oz) butter
Grated rind ½ lemon
175g (6oz) dark brown sugar (Barbados)
1 tablespoon black treacle
6 eggs (beaten)
2 tablespoons brandy or rum

Oven temp. 180°C/350°F/gas mark 4

ROYAL ICING

Start with 250g (½lb) icing sugar to one egg-white and add more of either as necessary to achieve the consistency you require – the smaller the icing tube the runnier you will need it. I throw mine in the Magimix and it mixes beautifully, with the great advantage that the lid stops the icing sugar flying all over the room, but if you aren't lucky enough to have one of these then either an ordinary mixer or a wooden spoon will do a perfect job. To colour royal icing just add a few drops of colouring into the icing while mixing it.

TRAGACANTH ICING

This is royal icing with a little gum tragacanth added, which makes the icing much harder when dry. Just beat in ½ teaspoon of gum tragacanth to every 4 heaped tablespoons of icing before you use it. Gum tragacanth can be bought from a chemist or ordered by post.

WATER ICING
Just add water to some sieved icing sugar until the desired consistency is reached.

TOFFEE GLASS (for swimming pool)
Heat 250g (½lb) granulated sugar in 150ml (¼pt) water until the sugar is dissolved then bring to the boil. Boil until you reach the 'soft-crack' stage, or until just before the mixture starts to colour, then remove and use immediately. I think a sugar thermometer is really worth having for this – all that business of dropping bits into cold water or onto saucers is rather haphazard.

FOOD COLOURINGS
I have used a selection of basic colours, plus the more unusual black, brown, gold and silver (the last two taste revolting but are completely non-toxic). Mary Ford stocks all these, and her whole range of colours is delightful – including her flesh colour which is much better than an ordinary pink for faces etc.

CANDY CANES
Used in Four-poster, can be bought at Harrods.

RICE PAPER
Buy in sheets from any good stationer, or order by post.

LACE EDGINGS, TUDOR ROSES, BOWS ETC
These can be very useful for decorating all sorts of cakes. For the lace and the roses, draw the shape required on a piece of paper, slide it under a sheet of Bakewell paper, and pipe over the design with royal icing and a no. 1 (lace) or no. 2 (roses) tube. Slide the design along and repeat as necessary. For the bows used in the cradle and Valentine I used a no. 5 tube and pink royal icing.

ROSES AND IRIS

Colour 1 packet of fondant as required (makes about sixteen roses) and keep in a plastic bag while you are working. Make a cone shape. Take a further small piece of fondant, flatten between thumb and forefinger into a thin petal shape, moisten with water and wrap around cone (fig. 4).

Make another slightly larger petal and wrap around the opposite side (fig. 5).

Continue to build up the rose with further petals, increasing their size gradually. Curl over the tips of the petals gently with a finger (fig. 6).

When the rose is complete, squeeze the underneath into a neat shape, twisting and pulling until the unnecessary icing comes away. Leave on Bakewell paper to dry (figs. 7, 8, 9).

To make buds stop at the stage of fig. 6.

To make iris colour about ¼ packet of fondant purple (makes four complete iris). Make 12 individual iris petals and leave to dry, curled over a rolling pin (fig. 10).

When dry, fix iris petals together with a little green fondant, holding in place for a few minutes until they are firm enough to stand upside down on their own to dry (figs. 11, 12).

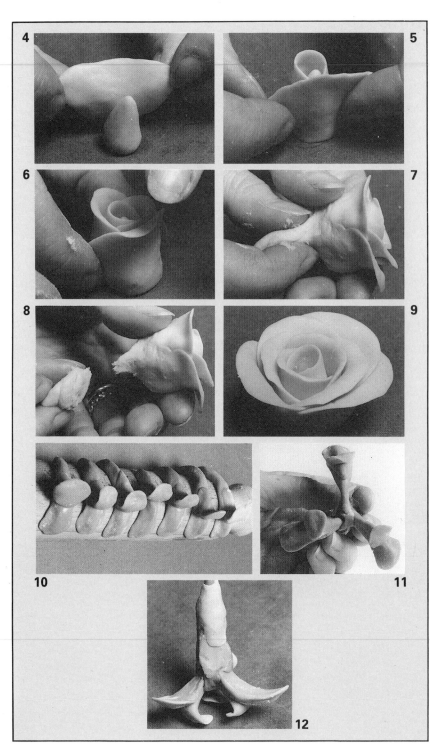

ADDRESSES

All icing equipment and edibles, including black, brown, silver and gold colourings
Mary Ford, Cake Artistry Centre Ltd, 28, Southbourne Grove, Bournemouth BH6 3RA Tel: (0202) 422653 & 431001

All icing equipment and edibles, including the fondant used throughout this book
Baker Smith Ltd, 65, The Street, Tongham, Farnham, Surrey GU10 1DE Tel: (02518) 2984

Candy canes
Harrods Ltd, Brompton Road, London SW1 Tel: (01) 730 1234

Tala icing bags and tubes
John Lewis and branches.

Thin candles
Called 'Les Petites Folies'. I found them in General Trading Co, 144 Sloane Street, London SW1 Tel: (01) 730 0411 but may be available elsewhere.

SLEEPING BEAUTY

I originally made this cake for Millie Fox's sixth birthday. Her parents, Edward and Joanna, are both actors, and as she herself has a strong sense of the theatrical I thought she'd like a cake with some sort of story to it. Nursery rhymes and fairy stories are very good sources of inspiration for children's cakes and if it's a child you don't know very well it's always worth asking if they have a particular favourite.

Children's birthday cakes must, of course, have candles, and it can be quite difficult incorporating them in the cake without spoiling it, so I always try to think of a way of bringing them in as part of the design. A wedding cake pillar stuck with candles makes quite an attractive candelabra and can be used in various different ways – in this case I think it helps the medieval feeling.

It does seem unfair to eat Sleeping Beauty before the Prince arrives, but on the other hand to wait a hundred years might make the cake a little over mature.

Medium difficulty
Start two days before

INGREDIENTS
(see pp. 8 to 14 for details)

1 loaf-tin cake
1 packet marzipan
1 packet fondant icing
1 25cm (10″) square cake board
250g (½lb) royal icing
4 Tudor roses and sheet edging
numbers 2, 35 and 5 icing tubes
food colourings, including gold and
    silver
1 wedding cake pillar
candles
Bakewell paper

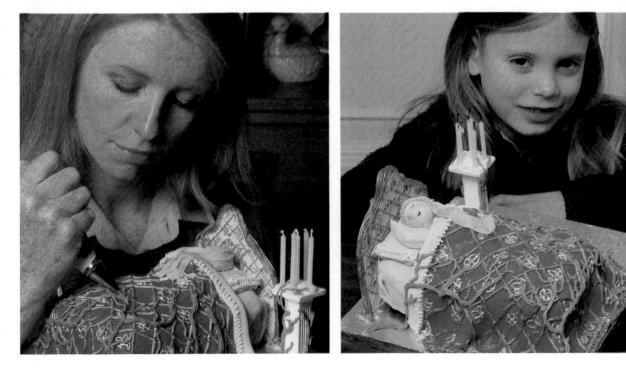

Using the cake right-side up, cut away some of the top to leave roughly the shape of a person asleep, ignoring the head and neck. Cover with marzipan (fig. 1).

Cover the end of the bed where the pillow will be with white fondant, and, using the cake as a guide, draw the shape of a bedhead onto a piece of paper (fig. 2) and cut it out. Roll out some white fondant and, using your paper pattern, cut out the shape of the bedhead. Leave on Bakewell paper for a day or two to dry thoroughly.

Colour a little of the fondant pink, and model a head and arm (fig. 3). Leave on Bakewell paper to dry.

Make a suitably sized pillow in white fondant and while still soft make a dint with your finger-tip for the head, and mark creases with a cocktail stick (fig. 4).

Put the cake on one side of the board and place the pillow, head and arm in position (fig. 5).

Keeping back a little for the sheet and candelabra, colour the remainder of the fondant red. Quickly drape it over the bed and make some folds with your fingers before trimming it evenly round the edges with a sharp knife. Fold a strip of white fondant over the edge as a top sheet (figs. 6, 7, 8).

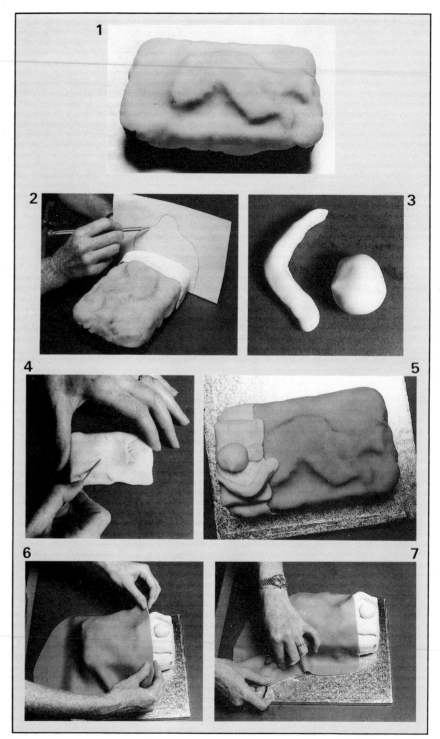

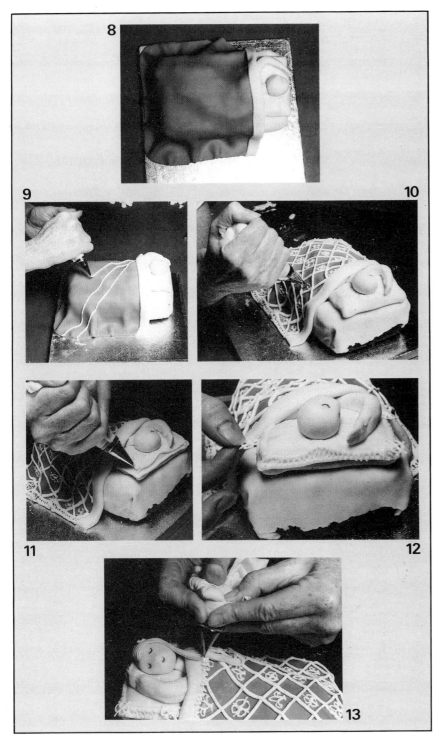

With a fine brush, paint closed eyes in blue and a little pink mouth. Using no. 2 tube and white royal icing pipe diagonal lines criss-crossing over the bed cover (fig. 9).

Fill in alternate squares with suitable motifs – (I've used Tudor roses and fleurs-de-lys) (fig. 10). Decorate the bedhead similarly.

Again using the no. 2 tube and white royal icing, pipe round the edges of the pillow and top sheet and while still wet press trimming onto sheet and Tudor roses onto pillow (figs. 11, 12).

With no. 35 tube, and yellow royal icing pipe some long golden hair (fig. 13).

When all the icing is dry, paint the decorations with gold, silver and bright colours to make the cover and bedhead look as rich and royal as possible. Stick the bedhead into position with royal icing. Put a lump of white fondant on top of the pillar, push a suitable number of candles into it, and stick the pillar next to the bed. Finally, using no. 5 tube and a leafy-green royal icing, pipe encroaching vegetation all over the bed and candelabra.

*SCRABBLE

The original of this was one of the first cakes I ever decorated. It was made for my sister Clare, who was quite a Scrabble fanatic at the time, and is a very simple and effective cake to do. In those days I hadn't discovered fondant icing or black or brown colouring, and I remember the top being coated in extremely bumpy royal icing and the letters being made out of rather crumbly marzipan, painted with cochineal. But we all thought it looked wonderful at the time, and no doubt the appreciation that the family showed me gave me the support I needed to go on experimenting. Knowing the amount of mess I have to clear up now when I have finished decorating a cake, I realise how tolerant my mother must have been to put up with my teenage sticky efforts.

It's great fun positioning the letters, and the cake can obviously be made for many different occasions as long as the recipient is a Scrabble player. A crossword would be another similarly effective way of writing a message.

Easy
Start day before

INGREDIENTS
(see pp. 8 to 14 for details)

1 baking tray cake
2 packets marzipan
1 to 2 packets fondant
food colourings
1 40cm (16″) square cake board

*SCRABBLE is a Registered Trade Mark

21

Turn the cake upside-down and cut to a perfect square (figs. 1, 2).

Cover with marzipan (fig. 3). Let dry a little.

Cover neatly with white fondant, starting with the sides so that the top has no joins. Let dry. Using a real Scrabble board as a guide, rule lines criss-cross onto the cake with dark brown colouring (fig. 4).

Colour the remaining fondant beige, roll and cut from it about sixty squares to make the letters. Make four letter racks from marzipan. While they are drying paint the details on the cake (fig. 5).

Paint the letters. Put the cake on the board and stick the letter racks in position. Stick letters into a suitable message, and remainder onto racks.

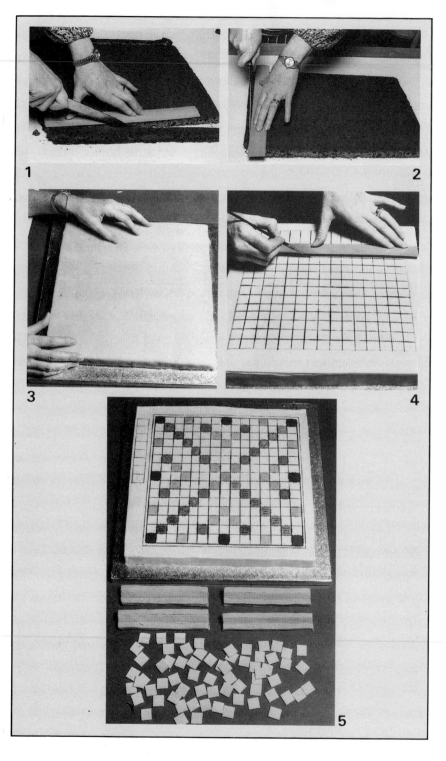

First Bake
your cake

SNAIL

When we were on holiday at Kimmeridge Bay, Dorset a few years ago, we collected a bagful of beautiful snail shells which I have kept in a cupboard in the kitchen ever since. Every year towards Christmas I imagine myself getting well ahead with the preparations and sitting down on Christmas Eve to arrange them into some sort of wonderful centrepiece for the table, and every year I let myself down and have the usual rush of last-minute shopping and cooking and end up sticking a few sprigs of holly into a bowl. But at least the shells did give me the idea for this cake which I made for Jill Townsend's little boy, Luke, who hated school at the time (creeping like snail unwillingly etc). It would do equally well as a hint to a friend who was being slow about something.

Try to find a real shell to copy, or at least a very good photograph, for as usual with something from Nature, the real thing is far more beautiful than anything one could design oneself.

And this Christmas I really will start everything early. . . .

Medium difficulty
Start day before

INGREDIENTS
(see pp. 8 to 14 for details)

1 20cm (8") round cake
small amount of extra cake, any flattish shape
2 packets marzipan
1½ packets fondant icing
2 thin candles
Bakewell paper
non-toxic plasticine
food colouring

Cut a slice off the circumference of the cake so that it will stand on its side (fig. 1).

Using this piece plus the extra cake, cut a slug-like shape for the body (fig. 2). Stick the pieces together with a little marzipan.

Cover with marzipan, extending and raising one end for the head. Put a piece of plasticine under the head to keep it raised until it has dried (fig. 3). Leave on Bakewell paper.

Colour the half-packet of fondant a snailish brown-black (see p. 11) and cover the body. Stick the two candles in the head for antennae (fig. 4).

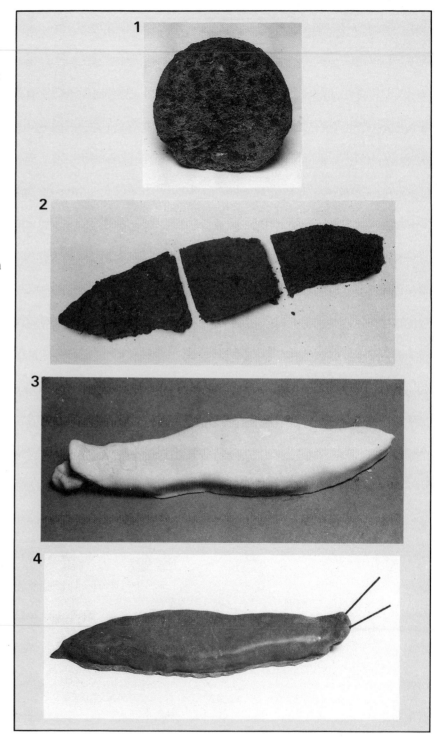

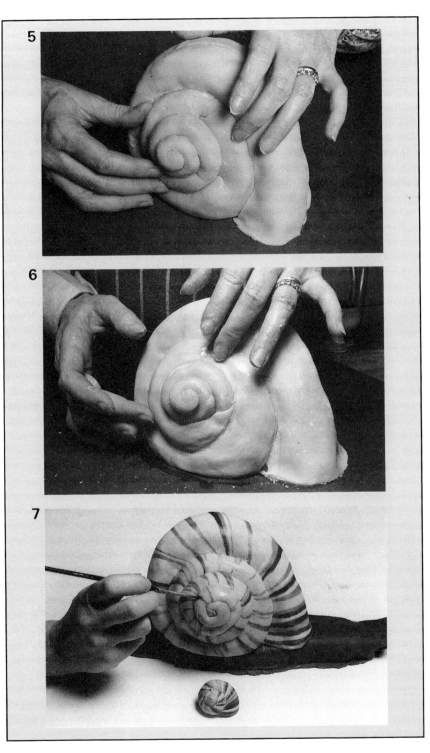

Cover the shell with marzipan, smoothly on one side and creating a spiral with a roll of marzipan on the other (fig. 5).

Colour the rest of the fondant yellow (see p. 11) and cover the shell with it, in pieces if necessary, smoothing and blending into shape with wet fingers (fig. 6).

Stick the shell onto the body with a little fondant, and using your real shell as a guide, paint with stripes (fig. 7).

DARTBOARD

The longer my brother Peter lives in Los Angeles the more nostalgic he becomes for typically English things. At one stage whenever we visited him we had to load our cases with Marmite, baked beans, chocolate and all sorts of other things that apparently just aren't the same over there (there is now a special shop specifically catering to local English cranks). You can't get much more English than a game of darts in a pub, which is something he always wants to do when he comes home; he now even has a dartboard hanging on the wall of his house in California. So it was easy to choose this design of cake for his last birthday. I stuck the darts in the numbers to make his age of course.

Up till now I've never had much interest in the game, but together with millions of others I have been watching the recent televised darts matches. As with *Pot Black* and *One Man and his Dog*, I have found myself absolutely fascinated by a sport I would never have thought could have any interest for me.

Easy
Start day before

INGREDIENTS
(see pp. 8 to 14 for details)

1 baking tray cake
1 35cm (14") round cake board
1 to 2 packets marzipan
2 packets fondant icing
3 cocktail sticks
number 3 tube
250g (½lb) royal icing
Bakewell paper
food colourings, including gold and
    silver

Turn cake upside-down. Using the cakeboard as a guide, cut a circle from it with a sharp knife (fig. 1).

Trim 5mm (¼") from the edge, to allow for the width of the icing. Put on to the board and cover with marzipan (fig. 2).

Cover with fondant, starting with the side so that the top has no join (fig. 3).

With a brush dipped in brown food colouring mark out the two circles, using a real darts board as a guide; (I used a cake board and a large saucer) (figs. 4, 5).

With a ruler divide the circles into twenty segments and then, again following the real board, paint with appropriate colours. Paint the outside edge silver. Allow to dry (fig. 6).

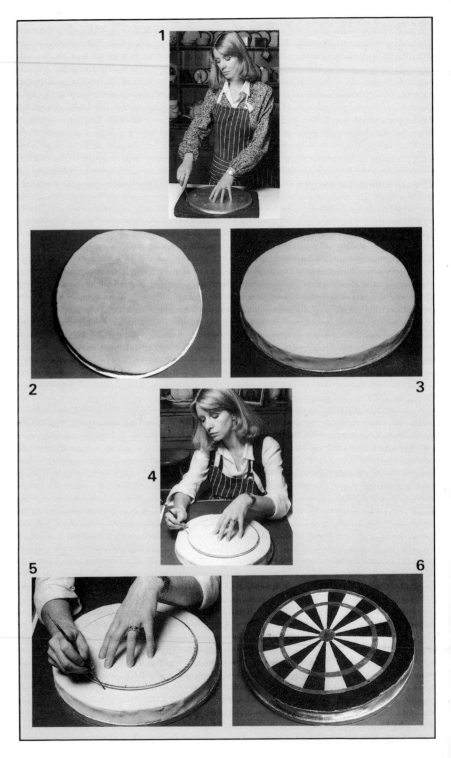

Meanwhile make the darts. Mould a lump of fondant around each cocktail stick, leaving the ends sticking out. Roll and cut out of fondant twelve flights, marking them gently with a knife to look like feathers (fig. 7).

Leave the flights to dry on Bakewell paper and push the darts into a lump of plasticine so that they dry upright.

With the no. 3 tube and royal icing, pipe the metal grid onto the board. This is much easier if you have a turntable. Start with the circles, turning the cake with your free hand (fig. 8).

Then pipe the radial lines and finally the numbers, copying the real board all the time (figs. 9, 10, 11).

Stick the flights onto the darts (fig. 12). Let dry. Paint the piping on the board silver and paint the darts red and gold. With a cocktail stick dipped in very hot water make three holes in the board for the darts in the appropriate numbers and stick them in with a little royal icing.

31

DRACULA'S TOMB

Hallowe'en is a wonderful opportunity for cake making. Witches, ghosts, goblins – now that there is a black food colouring available there is no end to the possibilities. I made this cake for my daughter's current fiancé (age 7) who was delighted with it and I think found it suitably nasty – he was particularly impressed with the dripping blood.

I came across the marbling effect on the tomb quite by chance – I was kneading some colour into a piece of fondant for another cake, and when it was half mixed it struck me how like marble it looked. I'm sure I shall use it in all sorts of other designs now.

If you do make this cake please be very careful to remove the cocktail sticks when cutting it up. I did the most terrible thing once when cooking a duck for my brother-in-law Gordon: I had no skewers in the kitchen and after stuffing the bird I secured it with pins, being certain that I would remember to take them out afterwards. It wasn't until Gordon found one in his mouth that I remembered. Thank heavens he wasn't hurt, but as I wasn't sure exactly how many I'd used, it did give the rest of the meal a certain tension – and certainly taught me a lesson.

Difficult
Start three days ahead

INGREDIENTS
(see pp. 8 to 14 for details)

1 loaf-tin cake
1 packet marzipan
1½ packets fondant icing
3 cocktail sticks
125g (¼lb) royal icing
green, black, silver, gold and red food colourings
number 1 icing tube

33

Turn cake upside-down. Cut and scoop out the centre, to a depth of about 5mm (¼"). Cover neatly with marzipan, making sharp corners. The scooped out centre need not be covered (fig. 1).

Mix a little green colouring into the 1 packet white fondant, kneading it rather briefly so as to leave a marbled effect. Keeping back a little for the mouldings roll it out and cover the cake. Measure the top and cut a lid the correct size. Leave it to dry on Bakewell paper for a couple of days (fig. 2).

Meanwhile mould a head and hands from about ¼ packet of white fondant. Push a cocktail stick into the neck and let dry a little by standing in a piece of plasticine. Colour the remaining fondant black (see p. 11). Roll and cut a cloak collar and wrap it round his neck. Give him two fangs and paint black hair and eyes (fig. 3).

Cover inside of tomb with black fondant.

Cut mouldings out of remainder of marbled fondant and stick to tomb and lid, rounding the edges with thick strips (fig. 4).

Make a nameplate for the front and while still soft mark name with a cocktail stick (fig. 5).

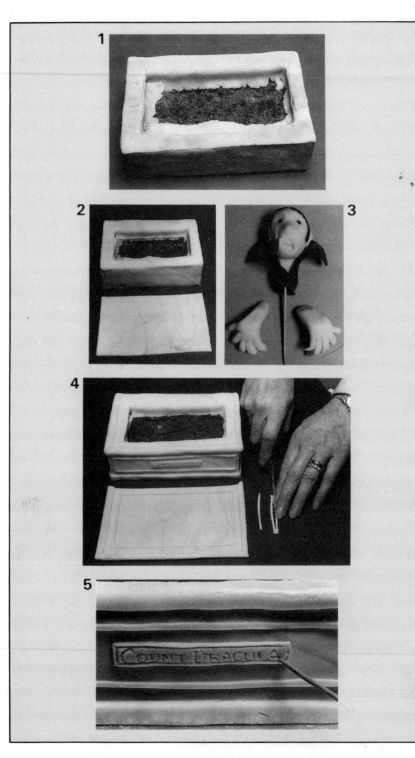

34

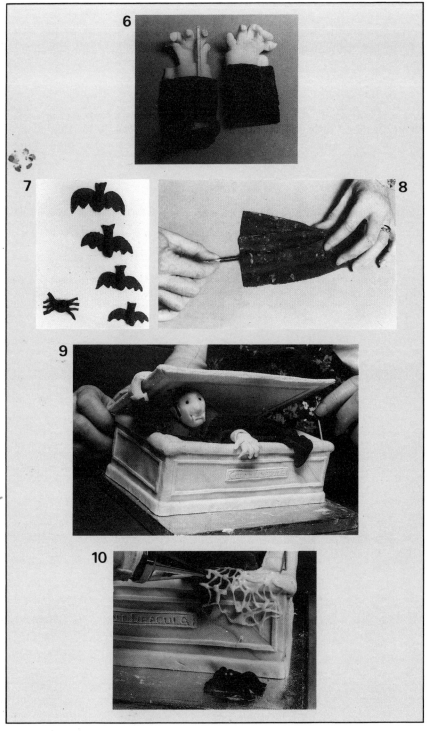

Put white cuffs round the hands. Place a cocktail stick on one hand and then wrap black sleeves around both as shown (fig. 6).

Model some bats and a spider out of black fondant and leave to dry on Bakewell paper (fig. 7).

Stick the head still on its cocktail stick into the tomb. Stick the left hand gripping the front and the right hand on its stick upright in the side (see colour photo for position). Roll and cut a rectangle of black fondant for the cloak. Quickly make folds with a pencil or the handle of a brush (fig. 8).
    Wrap around the neck, covering ends of sleeves and draping over the edge of the tomb.

Stick lid in position, resting it on the stick hidden in the hand and on his head. Prop up temporarily with a cocktail stick at the other end. Leave to dry (fig. 9).

With a no. 1 tube and white royal icing, put the cuff-links and rings onto Dracula, eyes on the spider, and a web on the front of the tomb (fig. 10).

When all is dry, paint rings and cuff-links gold, nails and mouth green. Put a little red round the eyes and on the fangs and let it 'drip' onto the tomb. Paint web silver. Stick on spider and bats (I only used two) with a little icing. Finally remove supporting stick.

35

GRANDFATHER CLOCK

I think this makes a lovely cake for a grandfather's birthday: unless it's someone who's very sensitive about their age you can point the hands to the relevant numbers – eighty-four in this case. This is the first time I have tried this design and I wasn't at all sure if I could make it stand up. I decorated the whole thing horizontally and then when it was completely dry we all held our breath while I gently tilted it to the upright – and it did stand beautifully. If you're nervous you could always put a table against the wall and stand the clock on it, leaning slightly onto the wall, which after all is what a real grandfather clock usually does, but I think you may find it will not be necessary.

Difficult
Start three days ahead

INGREDIENTS
(see pp. 8 to 14 for details)

1 23cm (9″) square cake
250g (½lb) royal icing
1 to 2 packets marzipan
1 to 2 packets fondant icing
numbers 1, 2 icing tubes
1 15cm (6″) square cake board
brown, black and gold food colourings

Cut the cake into three sections. These will make the centre, top and bottom of the clock (fig. 1).

Stick these firmly together with royal icing (fig. 2).

Cut the top into a decorative shape, then cover the whole clock, including the 'back' (which at the moment is underneath) with marzipan. Allow to dry very thoroughly (fig. 3).

Colour most of the fondant brown (see p. 11) and cover the case with it. Cover the face with white. Let in small white shapes on front of case for decoration. Roll and cut out of brown fondant a door panel, a frame for the face and a panel for the base. Stick them on and add very thin strips of brown fondant for mouldings (fig. 4).

Mould two decorative pillars and four cones out of brown fondant. Stick onto top of clock and either side of face. Mark face by gently pressing an egg-cup onto the fondant. With a no. 1 tube and royal icing pipe squiggly decorations onto face and pillars, and a fine line along edges of clock and onto mouldings. With no. 2 tube pipe trellis-work onto sides and pipe hands onto face. When dry, paint decorations gold, including around face. Paint hands black (figs. 5, 6).

   Stand clock upright and stick to board with icing.

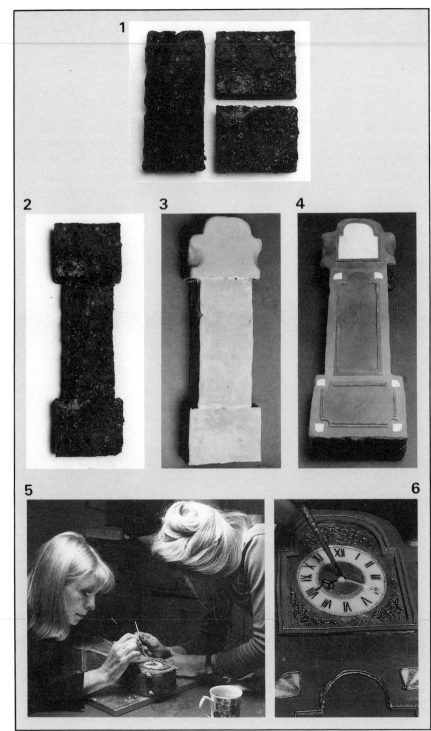

Mit your icing

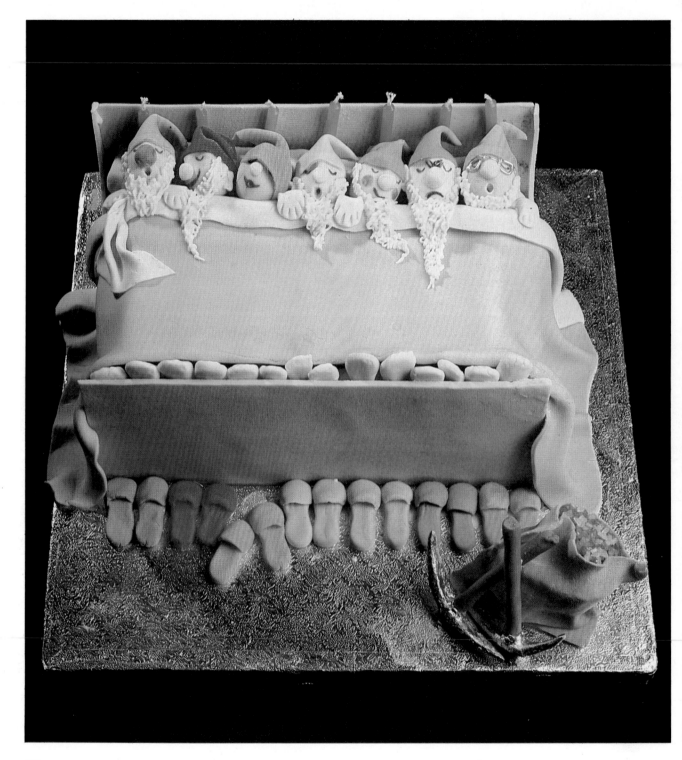

THE SEVEN DWARFS

This was a cake originally made for my daughter Katie for her seventh birthday. In that one, which she didn't see until THE DAY of course, all the dwarfs looked the same, but when re-making it for the book she confessed to me that she had really thought that they should all have their individual characters. I think it has added to it enormously. It's often worth asking the advice of someone of a similar age-group when making a cake for a child, as they usually have some very good ideas.

In this case it took the whole family, the photographer and a friend all thinking hard for quite some time before we could remember the names of all seven dwarfs.

Medium difficulty
Start two days ahead

INGREDIENTS
(see pp. 8 to 14 for details)

1 loaf tin cake
1½ packets fondant icing
1 25cm (10″) square cake board
seven chocolate finger biscuits
250g (½lb) royal icing
7 blue candles
number 1 icing tube
coloured coffee-sugar crystals
1 'Club' biscuit, or an extra chocolate finger in two pieces

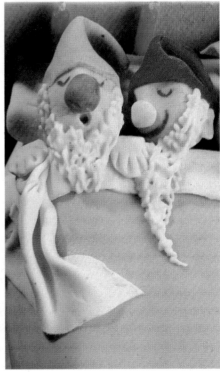

Colour ½ packet fondant blue (see p. 11) and, remembering you are using the cake widthways, measure and cut pieces to go at the head and the foot of the bed. Leave to dry on Bakewell paper. Colour about ¼ packet of fondant flesh pink and make seven little heads and seven pairs of hands and feet, bending hands ready to fit over the top sheet, and marking fingers and toes with a cocktail stick. Leave to dry on Bakewell paper (figs. 1, 2).

Cover the top of the cake with marzipan and using it widthways place the seven chocolate biscuits across the bed (fig. 3).

Colour some little pieces of fondant with various bright colours and wrap around the heads to make hats. Make a pair of slippers in the same colour for each dwarf. Colour a further small piece of fondant brown and make two pick-axes. When dry paint the tops silver. With a no. 1 tube and royal icing, paint glasses onto Doc. Check with an expert the expressions the various characters should have (fig. 4).

Paint the faces accordingly, including the glasses with silver (figs. 5, 6).

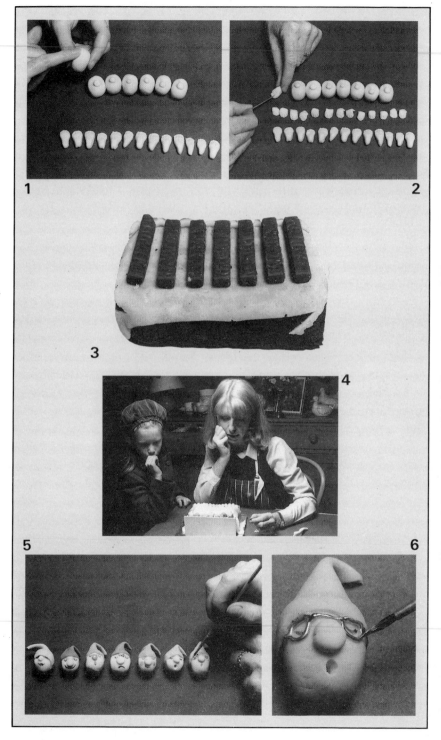

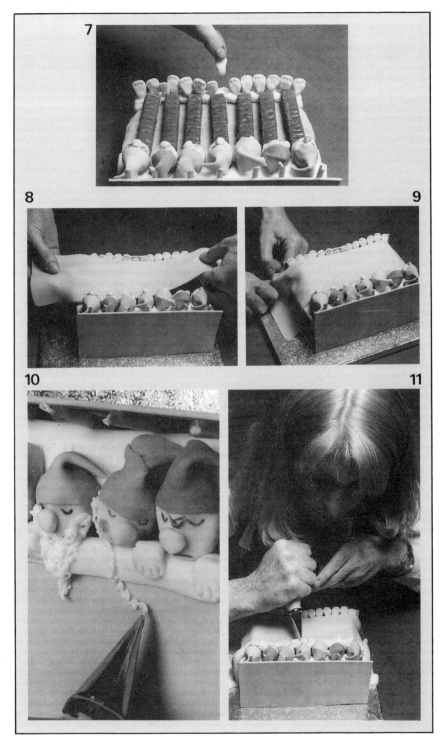

Make a long pillow out of white fondant and put it on the bed. Stick the headboard in position and carefully place the candles between this and the pillow. Put the heads on the pillow and stick the feet into a strip of icing at the other end (fig. 7).

Put the cake on the board. Colour about ½ packet fondant pink, and measure and cut a bedspread. Drape over the bed, making folds at the sides with your fingers (figs. 8, 9).

Fold a strip of white fondant over the top edge as a sheet, and give Sneezy a handkerchief. Stick the bottom of the bed in position and using a no. 1 tube pipe the beards and hair (figs. 10, 11).

Put slippers at the foot of the bed. Colour a small piece of fondant pale brown and wrap it around the biscuit to make a little sack. Put some icing in the top and fill with coffee-sugar 'jewels'. Stick pick-axes as if leaning against the sack.

TELEVISION SET

This was designed for my niece Sarah on her fourth birthday. When trying to think of ideas for a young child it often helps to imagine how they spend a typical day so that you can choose a design that will really mean something to them. Children's cakes are so often automatically made as boats, cars, numbers and so on without necessarily being particularly relevant to their life. Television, of course, is a pretty safe bet for almost any child nowadays and can also be a marvellous source of characters and ideas for other cakes. Do copy a real set when you make this – it will be far more authentic – and do choose a picture from a favourite programme, although I hope for your sake it's a cartoon: a portrait of Noel Edmunds or Brian Cant could be rather tricky!

The candles are incorporated by being the antennae – for Sarah's birthday I just doubled them up.

Easy
Start day before

INGREDIENTS
(see pp. 8 to 14 for details)

1 23cm (9″) square cake
1 to 2 packets marzipan
1½ packets fondant icing
2 or more thin candles
food colourings, including black and
**   silver**

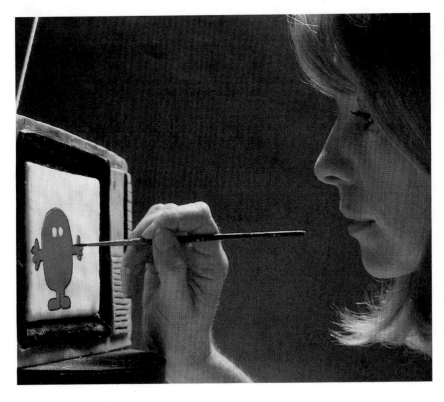

45

Cut away one side of the cake to make it rectangular (fig. 1).

Leaving an uncovered area for the screen, put marzipan on the flat bottom of the cake and on the sides. Turn it upside-down and pile up in pieces the cut off portion of cake to make the 'workings' at the back of the set (fig. 2).

Cover with marzipan (fig. 3).

Colour 1 packet of fondant red (see p. 11) and cover the whole TV with it except for the screen (figs. 4, 5).

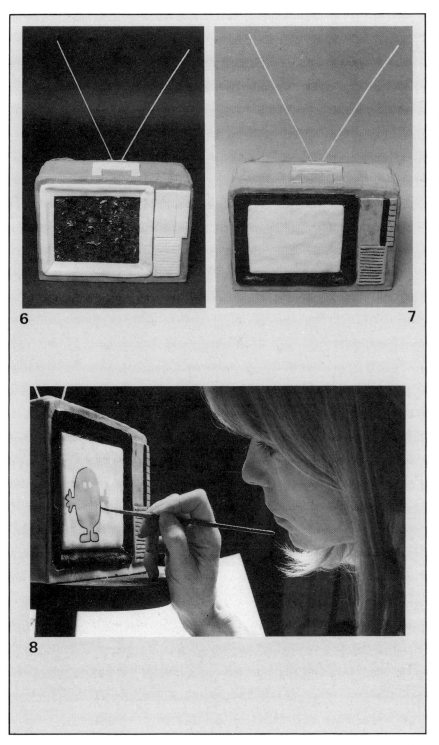

6

7

8

Cut a handle from white fondant and stick it on the top. Make a frame and a channel selector and stick them in position. Put in two candles as antennae (fig. 6).

Measure and cut a thick piece of white fondant for the screen and stick into place. Round the edges slightly with a finger-tip. When dry paint the frame, handle and channel selector in black and silver. Allow to dry (fig. 7).

When it is completely dry, paint a suitable picture on the screen with bright colours (fig. 8).

SWIMMING POOL

During last year my step-daughter Araminta went swimming so often that at times it seemed she was constantly in the pool. Whenever I pictured her I saw her like this – just a pair of legs disappearing into the water – so I had no problem in designing a cake for her.

The toffee-glass on top of the water to make it shine was a completely new idea I had never tried before, and I was very pleased with the way it turned out – it opens up all sorts of possibilities for other watery cakes. It did crystallise somewhat which in this case adds I think to the turbulent look of the water, but if you wanted it to remain clear then it might be better to use glucose instead of sugar.

Medium difficulty
Start day before

INGREDIENTS
(see pp. 8 to 14 for details)

1 loaf-tin cake
1 packet marzipan
1 packet fondant
250g (½lb) blue water icing
250g (½lb) granulated sugar and a little water, for toffee
food colourings, including silver
number 3 icing tube

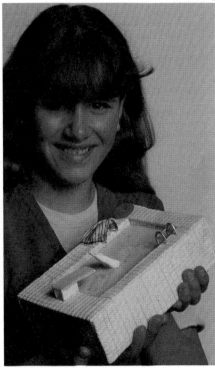

Turn the cake upside-down and trim the sides to make a neat rectangle. Mark another rectangle within this, slightly off-centre so as to have more width at the 'diving board' end. Criss-cross with a knife and remove carefully to a depth of about 15mm (¾″) (figs. 1, 2).

Cover the top and sides with marzipan, excluding the bottom of the pool (fig. 3).

Colour a small piece of fondant flesh pink (see p. 11), and make a pair of legs. Colour a further piece red for the ring, and make a towel and diving-board out of white. Leave on Bakewell paper to dry, creasing up the towel. With a no. 3 tube and royal icing, pipe side rails and rungs for the steps onto Bakewell paper. Leave to dry.

Colour the remaining fondant green and one by one roll out and cut suitably sized pieces to cover the marzipan. Mark into tiles with the edge of a ruler (figs. 4, 5).

As each is marked, stick into place until all sides are covered (fig. 6).

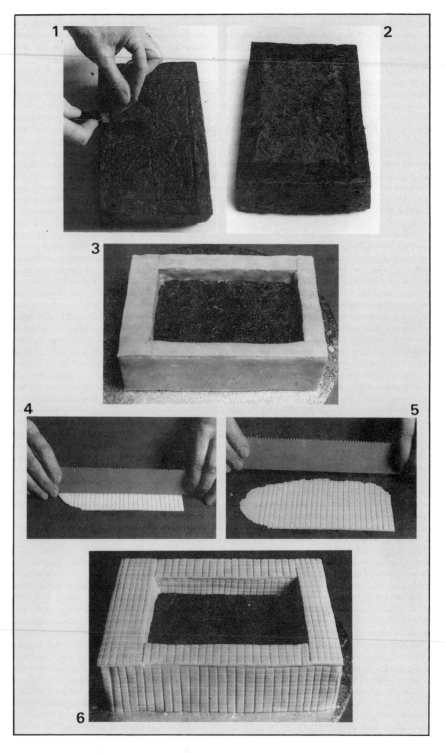

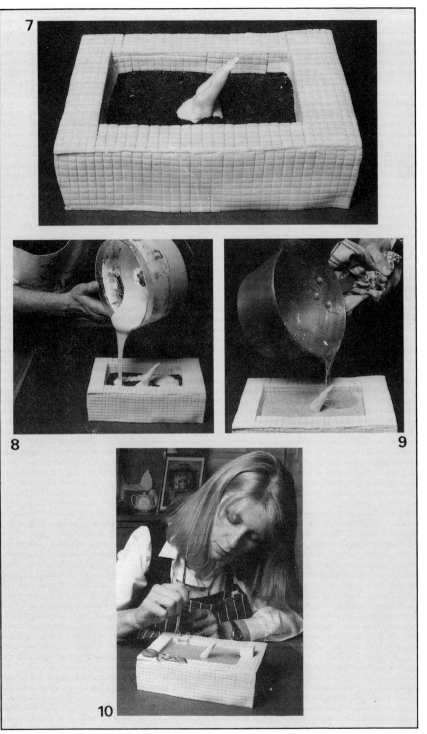

Fasten the legs securely to the bottom of the pool with a piece of fondant (fig. 7). Prop up if necessary until dry.

Mix the water icing and immediately pour into the pool (fig. 8).

When the icing is set, prepare the toffee and quickly pour a thin layer over the top (fig. 9).

Stick a little marzipan onto the diving board and mark herring-bone fashion with a knife. Paint the towel with stripes. When dry stick towel, ring, steps and diving board into position with a little icing. When dry, paint the steps silver (fig. 10).

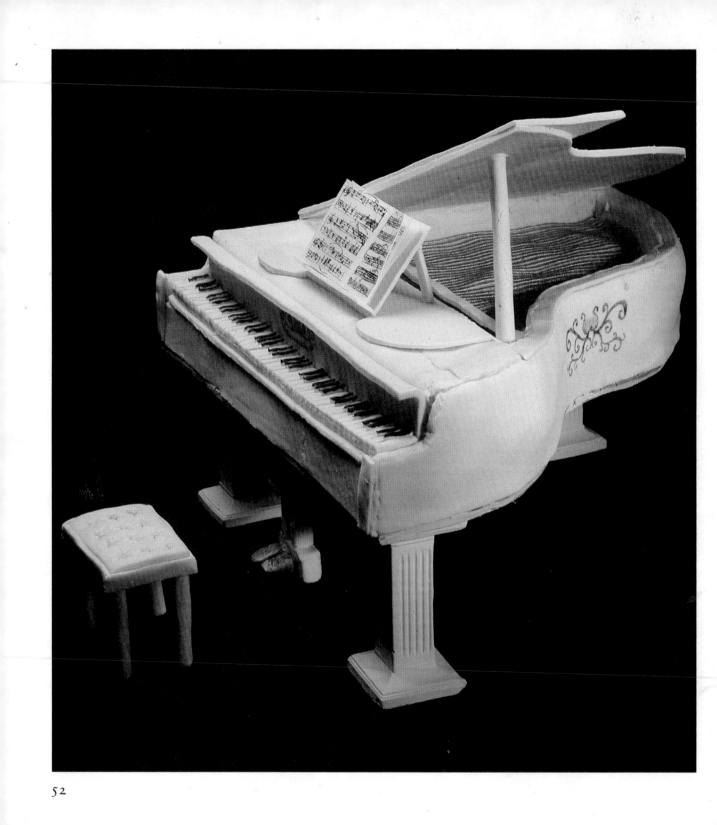

GRAND PIANO

This is one of my favourites and it's enormous fun to make. I originally did it for my mother who wanted a cake for a Summer Fair at the Royal Academy of Music where she taught for many years. That one was black, which seemed suitable for such a traditional institution, but this time I decided to lean more towards Liberace than Liszt and go all white and gold. Do remember that there is a cocktail stick inside the prop – if you included it in someone's portion of cake it could be extremely unpleasant.

You'll probably need a photograph of a piano to copy – we have an upright at home but I found it almost impossible to visualise the shape of a grand correctly without checking with a picture.

If you are good at painting in miniature you could even make the music have some special significance, and if it was for a birthday it would be lovely to make some tiny fondant candelabra with the thin candles.

Difficult
Start three days before

INGREDIENTS
(see pp. 8 to 14 for details)

1 23cm (9″) square cake
1 packet marzipan
1 30cm (12″) square cake board
Bakewell paper
1 to 2 packets fondant icing
250g (½lb) royal icing
numbers 2 and 1 icing tubes
gold and black food colouring
1 cocktail stick
rice paper
3 wedding-cake pillars

On a piece of paper the same size as the cake draw the outline of a grand piano, and using this as a guide cut the cake to this shape. Cut a step down for the keyboard. Cover sides and part of top with marzipan and allow to dry. Scoop out the body of the piano to a depth of about 5mm (¼″) and place on the board (fig. 1).

Cut a lid out of fondant, not forgetting the turned back piece at the front. Put on Bakewell paper to dry for a few days (fig. 2).

Cover the cake with fondant. Cut out a keyboard lid and sections for the music stand, and allow to dry (fig. 3).

Put a strip of fondant along the keyboard and cut into keys with a sharp knife. With royal icing pipe strings into the body and short notes onto the keys (in white at this stage) using nos. 2 and 1 tubes respectively. Make a music stool and legs, and allow to dry (figs. 4, 5).

Cover a cocktail stick with fondant and allow to dry (fig. 6). Paint the strings gold and the short notes black (fig. 7).

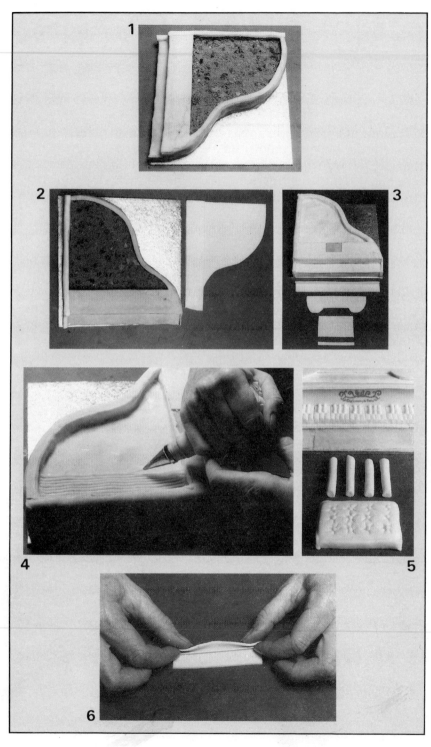

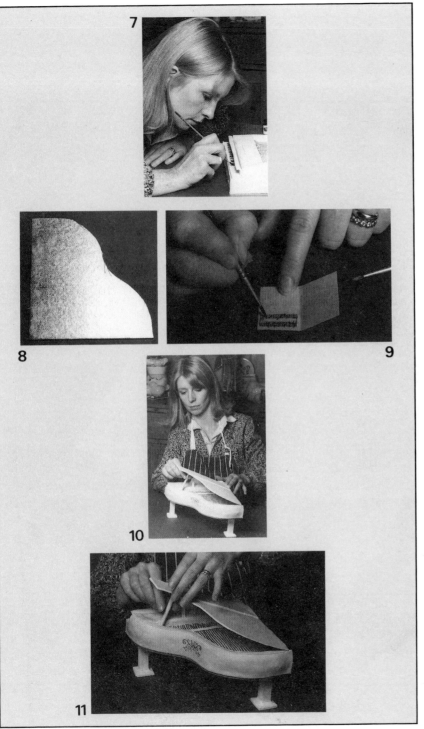

Trace round the cake onto the board, and cut out slightly smaller than the cake, so that the edges of the board will not show (fig. 8).

Cut several pieces of rice paper to the right size and paint one of them with music, using black colouring. Stick them together along a 'binding' line in the centre with a little royal icing (fig. 9).

Assemble and position music stand. Place cake on board and board on pillars sticking with a little royal icing. Carefully stick lid in position along 'hinged' edge and prop up. Assemble music stool. Decorate sides of piano and above keyboard with gold (figs. 10, 11).

CALCULATOR

To the modern schoolchild I suppose a calculator must seem as ordinary as a ruler did to me. It's always a good idea to think of something up-to-date for a cake design – only too often children's cakes, especially for boys, are based on the same old themes: boats, cars, football fields and so on. There must be many areas of the exciting modern technology that could be used for inspiration; perhaps a space-invaders cake – although as things are moving so fast no doubt that would look old-fashioned by the time the icing was dry. You could always put a tiny dot of icing on top of a cake and say it was a micro-chip – complete with its full circuitry of course.

Easy
Start day before

INGREDIENTS
(see pp. 8 to 14 for details)

1 shallow loaf-tin cake
1 calculator
1 packet marzipan
1 packet fondant icing
black food colouring

Trim the cake to a suitable shape and cover with marzipan (fig. 1).

Keep a calculator nearby for reference (fig. 2).

Colour about two-thirds of a packet of fondant grey (see p. 11). Roll it out and cut pieces to make a top and sides. Cut a hole out of the top which will let the marzipan show through as the display panel (fig. 3).

Allow the fondant pieces to dry for a few minutes before sticking in position. Cover the edges and corners with strips of white (fig. 4).

Cut squares of white fondant to make the keys and paint suitable figures (and/or letters) in the display panel (fig. 5).

Stick keys in position. When all is dry paint edges and corners black and, using calculator as a guide, paint the keys.

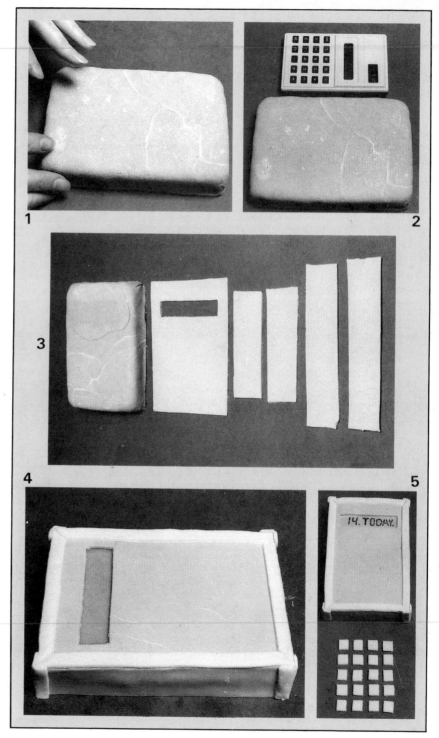

Improvise!

VALENTINE CARD

Strictly speaking this isn't a cake at all, but I have included it because it shows how useful fondant icing can be even on its own. You could make several greetings cards in this way and, with names piped on, put one at each place for a special tea party; or you could make a small one to decorate the top of a cake.

Again I have used the lace edging, which looks very pretty and delicate, and gives the card a Victorian look. If you are going to be decorating cakes fairly often it really is worth making quite a lot of it and storing it in an airtight tin – you can use it on so many things. Even stuck onto fancy biscuits it can look very effective.

Of course the identity of the sender of a Valentine Card is always a secret, but I think my husband may have had his suspicions when he received this one last year – I hardly think it could have come by post.

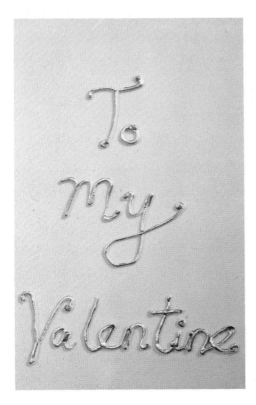

Medium difficulty
Start three days before

INGREDIENTS
(see pp. 8 to 14 for details)

1 packet fondant
royal icing lace edging
4 pink icing bows
250g (½lb) royal icing
125g (¼lb) flooding royal icing
Bakewell paper
numbers 3, 2 and 5 tubes
cocktail stick
pink, red, and silver colourings

Colour the fondant pink (p. 11) and roll and cut two rectangular pieces to a suitable size for a greetings card. Make two holes in each as shown (fig. 1).

With a no. 3 tube pipe greeting onto one of the pieces (fig. 2).

Prepare the royal icing lace and pink bows. With a no. 3 tube pipe an arrow in two pieces onto Bakewell paper making at least a couple of spares (fig. 3).

With the same tube pipe a heart shape onto Bakewell paper, of a suitable size to fit comfortably onto your card (fig. 4).

Colour the royal icing bright red and flood it into the heart as shown, easing it to the edges with the handle of a paint brush (figs. 5, 6, 7).

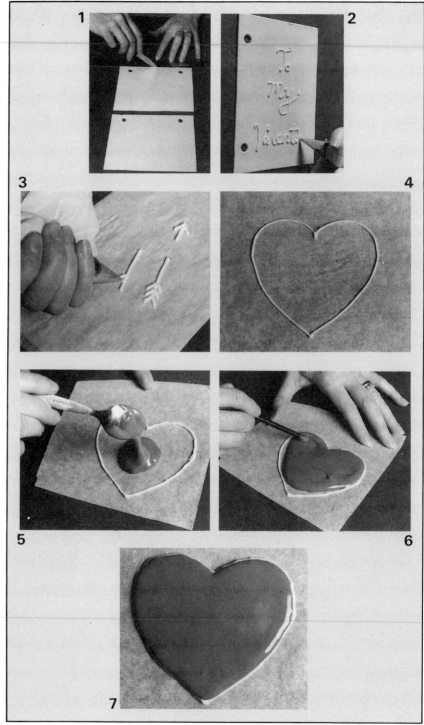

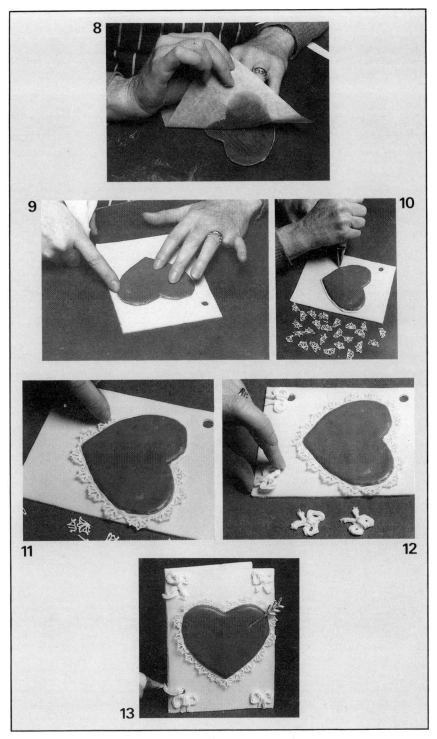

All these components must now be allowed to dry for two or three days.

Paint the arrows and writing silver when the heart is really hard, peel gently off Bakewell paper, and stick to the front of the card with a little icing (figs. 8, 9).

With a no. 2 tube and white royal icing, pipe around outside of heart and press lace gently into position, angled slightly upwards (figs. 10, 11).

Stick the four bows at the corners (fig. 12).

With a cocktail stick dipped in very hot water, make an indentation in the heart for the end of the arrow. Stick in place. Stand up the two pieces of card and join them together with royal icing and a no. 5 tube. Pipe ribbons through the holes (fig. 13). Finally stick the other piece of arrow in place.

FOUR-POSTER BED

I bought the candy-canes that make the posts of this cake some time ago without having any idea what I would use them for – they just looked as if they would come in very useful for something. When I was thinking of new cakes for the book I found them in a drawer and thought they looked very like wooden posts, and that led me on to the four-poster idea. Quite often a small ingredient can inspire a whole cake: I wonder if the designer of Trafalgar Square came across a wedding-cake pillar that morning?

This is not an easy cake to do, and when I started it I wasn't at all sure how it would turn out, or whether the roof would ever be strong enough to stay up, but finally I think it worked very well. The same method could be used to make roofs for all sorts of other cakes. If it's for a birthday then the best way of incorporating the candles would probably be as a candelabra (see Sleeping Beauty, page 16), and it would be more special if you made the lady in the bed look like the 'birthday girl'.

Difficult
Start at least three days before

INGREDIENTS
(see pp. 8 to 14 for details)

1 loaf-tin cake
1 packet marzipan
4 brown candy-canes
1 20cm (8″) square cake board
1½ packets fondant icing
Bakewell paper
lace for edging
250g (½lb) royal icing
numbers 9 and 2 icing tubes
food colourings including gold

Cut away some of the top of the cake to leave the rough shape of a person asleep (see Sleeping Beauty, p. 16) and cover with marzipan. Place on the cake board and stick the candy-canes firmly at each corner of the cake with lumps of fondant. Colour the ½ packet of fondant brown (see p. 11). Measure a rectangle slightly larger than that made by the four canes and cut a piece of the brown fondant to this size for the roof. Measure and cut another piece for the headboard and also four side pieces for the roof (fig. 1 – headboard not illustrated). Leave the pieces on Bakewell paper to dry thoroughly for two or three days.

Meanwhile cover the top end of the bed with white fondant for the undersheet. Make a pillow and a head (see Sleeping Beauty, p. 16), and put in position. Keeping back a little for the hair and top sheet, colour the remainder of the fondant yellow (see p. 11). Roll out enough to cover the top of the bed and drape into place, folding a strip of white fondant over the edge as a top sheet. Measure the height and length of the bed and add 5mm (¼") to the height and double the length. Cut a strip of yellow fondant to this measurement and quickly pleat finely with fingers and the handle of a paint brush (fig. 2).

Drape neatly into position on the side of the bed, pressing into a gather with your fingertip. Repeat for the other side and for the bottom of the bed (figs. 3, 4, 5, 6).

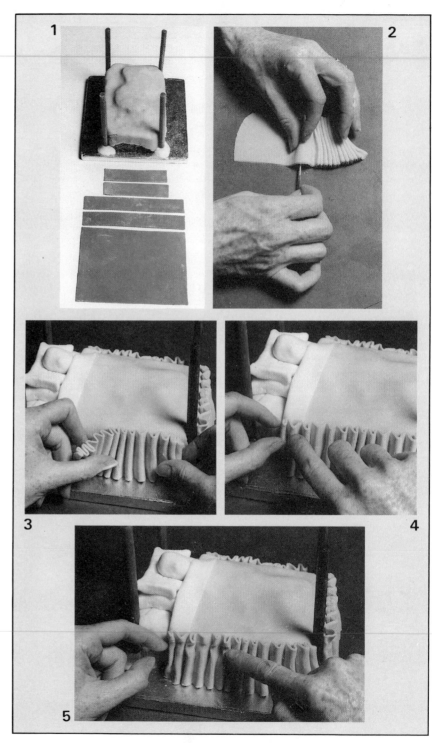

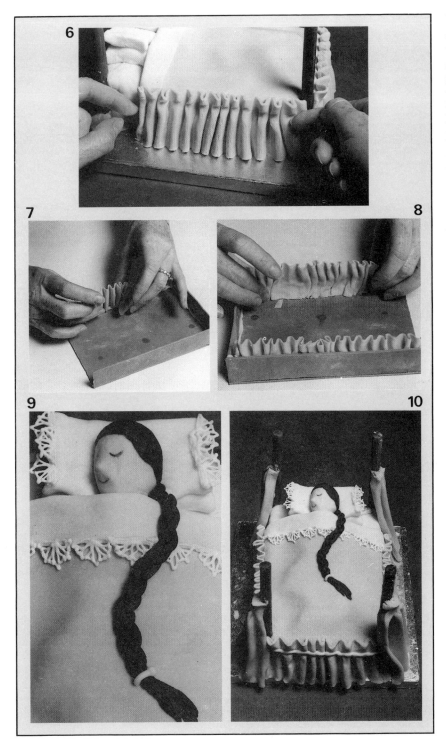

When the roof sections are completely dry and hard, assemble them carefully using royal icing to stick them together, and propping up with plasticine where necessary. Allow to dry and set thoroughly, then measure, cut and pleat three strips of yellow fondant in the same way as for the bed. Spread a little royal icing along the inside of the roof and press the curtains very carefully into place (figs. 7, 8).

Edge the pillow and sheet with lace (see p. 13). Colour the small piece of remaining fondant black (see p. 11). Cover the lady's head with a little of it then make a plait with three thin strips and fasten to the back of her neck. Paint eyes and a mouth (fig. 9).

One at a time, roll and cut curtains out of yellow fondant for the four corners, and drape onto the posts as shown, leaving the tops of the posts bare. With a no. 2 tube and royal icing, pipe trimming along the gathers of the bedspread, and a little band around the plait (fig. 10).

Stick the headboard and roof very carefully in position. One at a time roll and cut four more pieces of yellow fondant for the top of the posts. Stick them in place, tucking them inside the roof and gathering them with your finger at the join with the lower half (see colour pictures). With a no. 2 tube pipe ropes and hanging tassels round curtains and with the no. 9 tube decorate the roof as shown.

When all is dry and set, paint the piping in gold.

FAIRY PRINCESS

One of the exciting things about this cake is that when it has been eaten there is a real doll to keep. You could of course mould the head and body out of fondant, but it is much easier to use the doll and does make a lovely present. I made this originally for my daughter Katie's fifth birthday and when I re-made it to be photographed for the book we used the same doll, who inevitably had aged somewhat and needed a good deal of washing and tidying up. If you don't want to buy a new doll you could always use an existing one – perhaps there is a favourite who would love to be a princess for a day – but do make sure before you remove the legs that you will be able to put them back, or you could have a very miserable morning after!

Medium difficulty
Start day before

INGREDIENTS
(see pp. 8 to 14 for details)

1 pudding-basin cake
1 20cm (8") doll
250g (½lb) royal icing
1 packet marzipan
1 packet fondant
1 25cm (10") round cake board
silver balls
gauze
gold and silver colourings
numbers 3, 2 and 5 icing tubes

Clean up the doll if necessary and remove the legs, putting them in a safe place (figs. 1, 2).

With a no. 3 tube and a little white tragacanth icing (see p. 12), pipe a fairy wand onto Bakewell paper, making one or two spares. When dry paint silver (fig. 3).

Using the same icing and a no. 2 tube, pipe suitably sized wings onto the gauze and when dry cut out very carefully. With a little of the fondant make a crown to fit the doll, and when dry paint silver (figs. 4, 5, 6).

Cover the cake with marzipan and push the doll into the top (fig. 7).

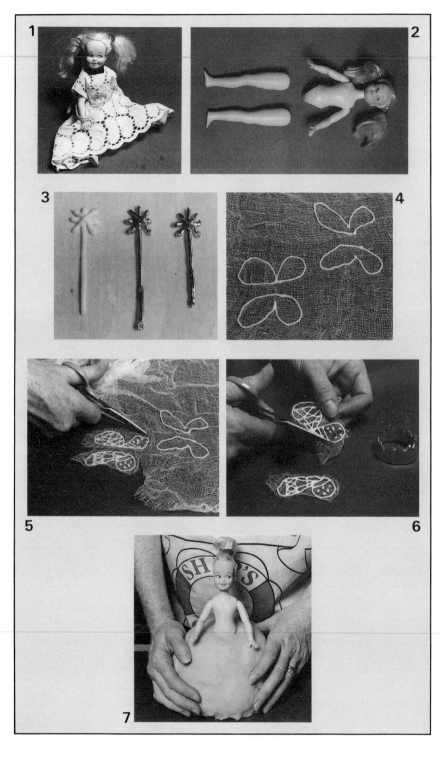

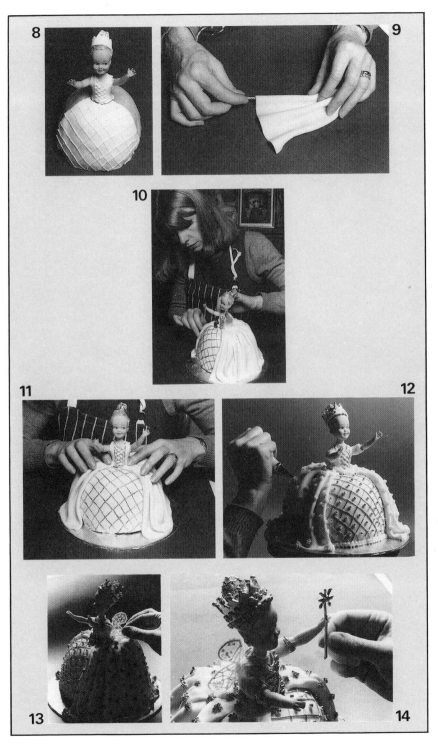

Cover the front of the skirt and the bodice with white fondant and with no. 2 tube decorate with white royal icing piped in a trellis (fig. 8).

Put the cake on the board. Measure the length of the skirt from waist to hem with a piece of string and add 2cm (1″). Roll and cut a piece of fondant to this width for the skirt. Quickly push into folds, using your fingertips and the handle of a brush (fig. 9).

Drape it onto the doll, adjusting the folds as you go. Repeat with enough pieces of fondant to make a generous skirt, folding in the side edges to disguise the joins. Push neatly in at the waist (figs. 10, 11).

Spread royal icing over her upper arms for sleeves. Pipe a net over her hair with a no. 2 tube. With dots of royal icing stick a silver ball into every square on the front panel and decorate the crown before sticking in position. Give her a little 'pearl' necklace and earrings. With no. 5 tube, pipe stars all over the skirt and with the same tube decorate the edges of the skirt, sleeves, bodice and waist (fig. 12).

When all the icing is dry, paint with gold and silver. Fasten on her wings with icing and stick her wand in her hand (figs. 13, 14). If you want birthday candles stick them onto the board around her, and they will light her up beautifully.

TYPEWRITER

I made this just because I liked the idea of doing a typewriter, but it would be ideal as a cake for an office party or for a secretary's birthday. The hardest work involved is in kneading the black colouring into the fondant, which is a long, messy job; apart from that it is a relatively simple cake to do but one which looks very effective. For once I don't necessarily recommend copying from the real thing – that is if you have a very up-to-date typewriter, as I think the more old-fashioned ones are better suited to this purpose. The modern 'golf-ball' and cartridge ones show so little of their mechanisms that they could look quite boring.

After searching the kitchen for something the right size to cut out the keys, I discovered that an eyeshadow stick in my handbag worked perfectly. I covered the eyeshadow itself with a tiny bit of Bakewell paper, (I neither liked the idea of eye-shadow on the cake nor fondant on my eyelids) and found I could then twist it up to push out the key I had just cut. So often if you improvise you can find the perfect equipment already existing at home.

Easy
Start day before

INGREDIENTS
(see pp. 8 to 14 for details)

1 20cm (8″) square cake
1 packet marzipan
250g (½lb) royal icing
1½ packets fondant icing
rice paper
food colourings, green, black, silver
numbers 35 and 2 icing tubes

Turn cake upside-down and cut away pieces to leave roughly a typewriter shape, sloping the key-board downwards (figs. 1, 2).

Cover with marzipan. With royal icing and a no. 2 tube, pipe the metal letters and their mechanism. When dry paint silver (fig. 3).

Colour 1 packet of fondant black (see p. 11). Roll out about half of it. Cover the keyboard and the back section of the typewriter. With the remainder make a roller and its ends and leave to dry on Bakewell paper (fig. 4).

Divide the ½ packet of fondant roughly into two and colour one piece pale green (see p. 11). Cut out space-bar, keys etc (figs. 5, 6 and see introduction).

Colour the remaining fondant a darker green. Roll out and measure and cut top, sides and front. Let dry slightly then stick in position. Type suitable message on rice paper and slip it under roller before sticking in position. With no. 35 tube pipe a royal icing 'bar' across paper and at joins of top and sides. When dry paint black. Paint keys with black figures and the ends of the roller with silver.

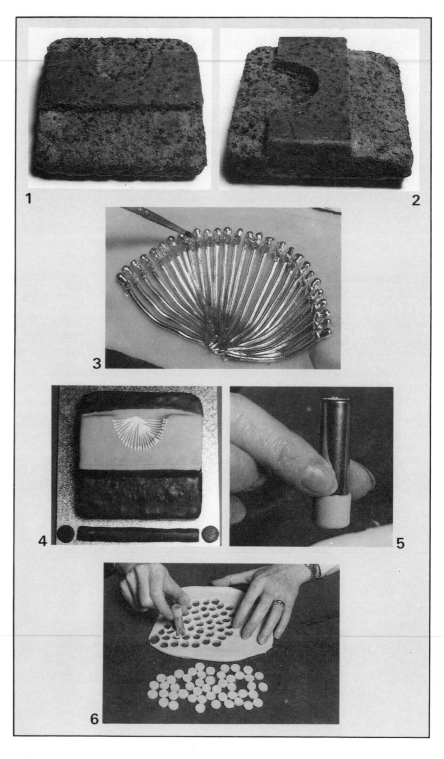

Not too
Ambitious

75

BABY'S CRADLE

I have now made this particular cake three times, and I am still very fond of the design. The first one was for my niece's christening. I had baked and decorated my sister's wedding cake a couple of years previously (covered in yellow roses and cameos depicting the couple's interests – see picture below) and wanted to use the top tier for the christening. She had stored it carefully in an airtight tin, and when I chipped off the old icing the cake underneath was beautifully fresh. It's a lovely tradition to use the wedding cake in this way, and does make it rather special – I only wish I had made yet another tier which I could have used for the christening of their second child, born last year.

The lace mantle is not easy to do, and it needs practice to be able to pipe the design quickly enough for it not to dry before draping it over the cake. Inevitably some of it will crack, but is quite easily touched up once in place. If it is a little boy's christening then obviously the pink icing should be replaced by blue.

Difficult
Start two days ahead

INGREDIENTS
(see pp. 8 to 14 for details)

1 15cm (6″) round cake
2 packets fondant icing
1 packet marzipan
1 piece of stiff wire, 8″ long
350g (¾lb) pink royal icing
Bakewell paper
gauze
250g (½lb) white royal icing
numbers 5, 35, 2 icing tubes
food colourings
1 20cm (8″) cake board

Cut sides off cake and scoop out the centre to a depth of about 15mm (¾″) (fig. 1).

Colour a little fondant pink and model a baby's head and arms. Leave to dry on Bakewell paper. Cover the cake with marzipan and let dry a little. Cover the top with white fondant, slitting it so that it fits down into the hollow as shown (fig. 2).

Measure the height of the cake and add 2cm (1″). Roll out a long strip of white fondant and cut it to this measurement widthways. Quickly pleat with fingers and a skewer (or handle of a brush) (figs. 3, 4).

Stick to side of cake with a little icing, draping attractively and allowing the top to stand proud of the cradle (fig. 5).

Mark an indentation along the gathering line (see Theatre Cake, p. 88).

Repeat with further strips of fondant until you have covered the sides, folding in the edges of each strip to disguise the joins. Make a little pillow of white fondant and place in the cradle.

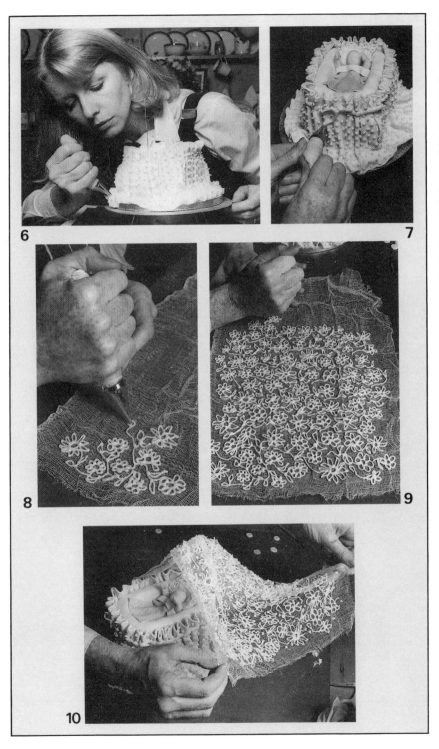

Position baby's head and arms and cover with a tiny pink fondant quilt (marked criss-cross with a ruler) folding a strip of white along the top edge for the sheet. Stick the wire into the cradle behind the baby's head and bend at a right angle 6cm (3″) from the protruding end. With a no. 2 tube and pink royal icing pipe dots all over the drapes (much easier on a turntable) (fig. 6).

Pipe trimming on top and bottom edges of drapes then change to a no. 35 tube and pipe a ribbon along the gathering line, making a bow at the front (fig. 7). Pipe another bow onto Bakewell paper and allow to dry. Paint hair and features on baby.

Drape the gauze over the wire and, allowing it to fall generously over each side, cut to the correct shape. Spread it out on Bakewell paper and with a no. 2 tube and white royal icing working as quickly as possible cover it with a floral lacy pattern (figs. 8, 9).

Before it sets drape it quickly over the wire, arranging into folds as you go (fig. 10). Repair any cracks.

Let it dry completely then with a no. 5 tube and pink royal icing pipe ribbon along edges and across top of wire. Stick bow into position.

TENNIS RACQUET

The world of sport offers a wealth of ideas for cakes, although
football fields have been rather over-exploited. This cake was made
for a friend of mine, Shirley Freeman, who is a very good tennis
player. Last summer I used to see her on the court first thing in the
morning as I walked through Battersea Park with the dog on the way
back from taking my daughter to school. When I was asked to make
her a birthday cake this immediately sprang to mind.

I considered at first just covering the cake in the centre of the
racquet with black fondant and then piping the strings onto it – you
could always do it that way if you're short of time or not feeling
particularly ambitious – but it does look marvellous with the strings
suspended in the middle of the racquet. If you do make it the way I
describe be sure to allow plenty of spare strings – I made three sets
and broke the first two before I got them in.

Difficult
Start two days ahead

INGREDIENTS
(see pp. 8 to 14 for details)

1 **baking tray cake**
1 **tennis racquet for cutting out**
2 **packets marzipan**
1 to 2 **packets fondant**
Bakewell paper
350g (¾lb) **tragacanth icing**
1 **75cm×38cm (30"×15") hardboard,**
   covered with green baize 'contact'
number 3 icing tube
food colourings

Carefully turn the cake upside-down. Place top of racquet on the cake, keeping it to one side as shown, and cut around the edge with a sharp knife as shown (figs. 1, 2, 3).

Then cut handle shape from remainder of cake. Stick the two pieces together with a little icing (figs. 4, 5).

Cover with marzipan, excluding centre of racquet. Leave to dry a little then cut out the centre (figs. 6, 7).

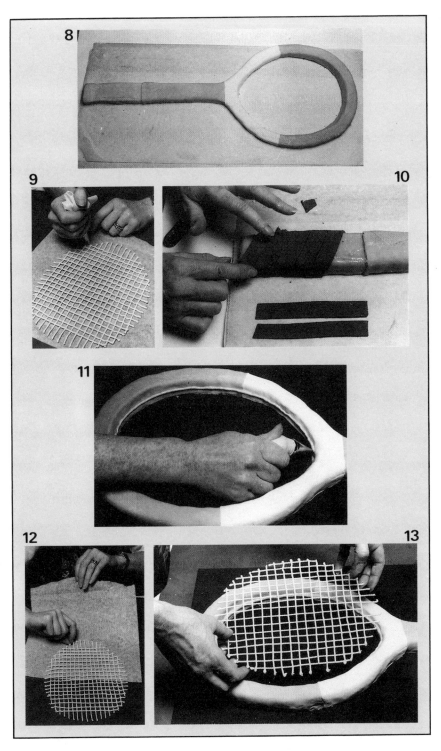

Use some of the spare cake to make the ball: squeeze it into shape with your hands and cover with marzipan. Leave to dry.

Colour about a third of the fondant beige (see p. 11). Set aside another third to be coloured red for the grip and leave the remainder white. Cover the racquet with the beige and white, leaving the grip uncovered (fig. 8). Cover the ball with white, marking two seams with a knife.

Cut a template to fit exactly within the centre of the racquet. Trace round this onto Bakewell paper. Mix and colour the tragacanth icing and using the no. 3 tube, pipe strings within the shape (don't forget your spares). Leave to dry for at least 24 hours (fig. 9).

Meanwhile colour a little fondant red and cut strips to cover the grip, using them diagonally (fig. 10).

When strings are completely dry slide the cake very carefully onto the board. With the same tube and icing as for strings pipe a line around the inside (fig. 11).

Lift the strings very gently off the Bakewell paper and place in position, repairing any broken edges with icing (figs. 12, 13).

Paint suitable greeting onto the racquet and grey seams onto the ball. Place ball on the board.

NEWS DIGEST
Currant affairs
Famous tenor says 'I cing again!'
Unions claim 'bigger slice of the cake'
Government says "We are raisin standards of living"
Flour-power back in fashion
Cake man sits on the board
THE FUNDAY TIMES
REVIEW
G.D. SCARFE
MY BROTHER G.S.
COLOUR MAGAZINE
THE HISTORY OF BIRTHDAY CELEBRATIONS
CAKE RECIPES
SPORT
ANOTHER GOAL REACHED
BUSINESS NEWS
ANNUAL INCREASE ANNOUNCED
STOCKS OF PRESENTS HIGH
HAPPY BIRTHDAY MR. SCARFE!
Gerry celebrates birthday today
by W. Nungar
TRAFFIC CAME to a standstill today
Lights switched on in Regent St.
by B. Wharton.
SPECIALLY designed birthday lights were
Weathermen say: 'Sunshine all the way'
by O. Figgs.
Gifts flood in
by C. Zuka
The ideal gift for him or her....
Gerald Scarves
In many different colours
Harrods

THE FUNDAY TIMES

My husband has worked at *The Sunday Times* as political caricaturist for many years, so when I gave a surprise party for him for his birthday some time ago I knew immediately what cake to do for him. The hardest work involved, of course, is in thinking of what to write on it and then in painting it all on in tiny letters, but at least it's only in a single edition and if you start early enough you should have more time to produce it than the journalists have for the real front page. It's great fun to do and very easy, and would be a good cake for anyone if you made all the headlines relevant.

Easy
Start two days ahead

INGREDIENTS
(see pp. 8 to 14 for details)

1 baking-tray cake
2 packets marzipan
2 packets fondant
black food colouring

Turn cake upside-down and cut to a rectangular shape (fig. 1).

Cover with marzipan (fig. 2).

Cover the sides with fairly thick fondant, and mark 'pages' on three sides with a ruler (figs. 3, 4).

Cover the top with a smooth sheet of fondant. Turn over two corners and put a little fondant underneath to cover the marzipan (fig. 5).

When the fondant is dry, using a real newspaper as a guide to type and layout, paint suitable words and pictures with black colouring (figs. 6, 7).

..... It's all worth it in the end.

THEATRE CAKE

I originally made this cake for a party to celebrate the end of a rather gruelling theatrical tour. The play was interesting to perform and the company was a happy one, but we did have some unsatisfactory theatres to play in. One in particular sticks in my mind which was really no more than a village hall. There were no wings, and the set was so wide and the stage so narrow that the only way for an actor to exit was to open a door at the side and leave the building entirely, racing along the street at the back of the hall when called on to re-enter from the opposite side. On our second night there it began to pour during act two, and we all got progressively wetter during the evening. As the play was a serious, tragic one it was difficult to keep a straight face when confronted by a dripping fellow actor who had ostensibly only been to another room in the castle.

It's not difficult to do, and what really makes it effective of course is the richness of the red and gold; it would make a very attractive centre-piece for the table at a theatre-lover's birthday party, or perhaps for an amateur dramatic society's first night celebration.

Medium difficulty
Start day before

INGREDIENTS
(see pp. 8 to 14 for details)

1 23cm (9″) square cake
1 25cm (10″) square cake board
2 to 3 packets marzipan
2 to 3 packets fondant icing
1 piece of extra cake for centre
250g (½lb) royal icing
numbers 35 and 2 tubes
red and gold colourings

89

Turn the cake upside-down and cover with marzipan (fig. 1).

Cover the centres of the sides with white fondant, (the corners will not show). Cover the top with a smoothly rolled-out sheet of fondant (fig. 2).

Roll out more white fondant and cut out the masks of comedy and tragedy. You will need two large ones for the centrepiece, and eight small ones for the sides, but as usual it is wise to make a few spares. Let them dry on any suitably rounded surface (I used a small spray-can and a thick crayon of my daughter's) (fig. 3).

Put the cake on the board. Colour a packet of fondant red (see p. 11). Measure the depth and width of one side of the cake and roll and cut a strip of red fondant to this measurement. Quickly pleat carefully with the handle of a brush and your fingers (fig. 4).

Stick to a corner of the cake, marking the gathering line with the brush-handle as shown (figs. 5, 6).

Repeat seven times for the other corners. Put the extra cake in the centre of the top, and cover with a small square of marzipan (fig. 7).

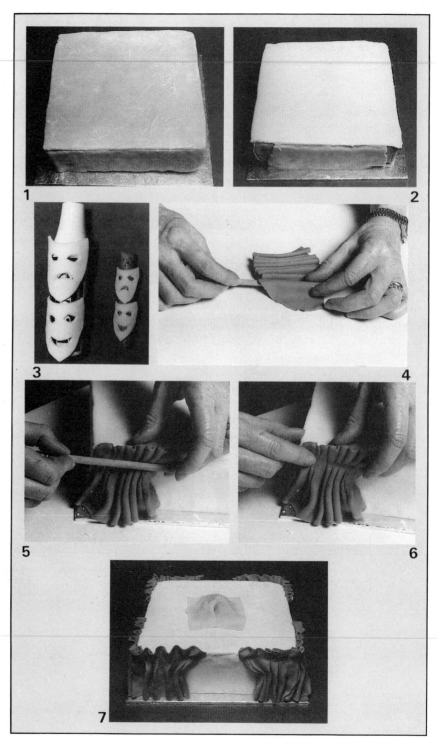

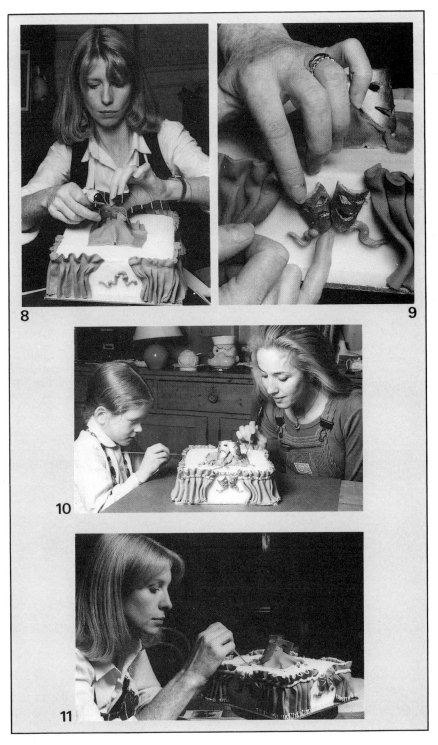

Cover this with red fondant. Colour a little of the royal icing red, and with a no. 35 tube pipe two ribbons at the centre of each side and four on the top, before positioning the masks onto them with a little more icing if necessary (figs. 8, 9).

With a no. 35 tube and white royal icing, pipe ribbon across gathers of curtains and along the gap at top of sides. With a no. 2 tube, pipe fringing along bottom of curtains and edge of centrepiece. With same tube pipe edging along top of curtains. When dry, paint all the white piping gold, using willing help if available (figs. 10, 11)!

8

9

10

11

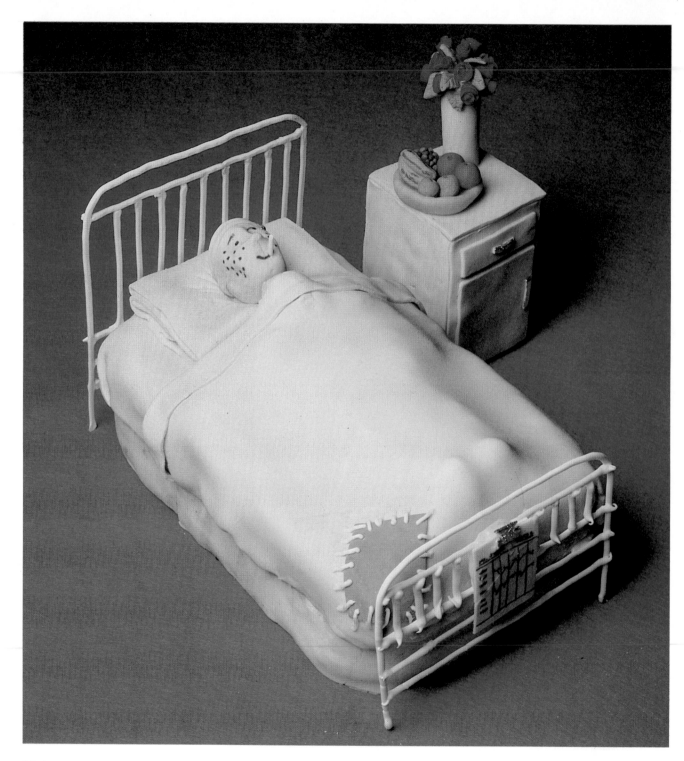

HOSPITAL BED

I designed this cake to be raffled at a fête in aid of a hospital. My first attempt at the patient was made out of much greener fondant and had a very gloomy expression. When I put him in the bed he looked so depressing that I thought it would quite put people off giving any money to the hospital so I quickly got out my red colouring and gave him his jolly smile and bright red spots.

The re-made cake for the book also had to go through some last minute adjustment: one of our three cats had obviously developed a taste for icing – probably from eating all the bits that had been falling on the floor during the course of preparing the book. I had been carefully putting the cakes into another room every evening and shutting the door, but inevitably one night it got left open and the cat took a mouthful off the corner of the bed–he also very neatly removed and ate all the noses off the Seven Dwarfs. Luckily as these cakes were made to be photographed and displayed no one will ever eat the icing, but even so it looked dreadful and there was no time to re-do the whole bedspread. So, as you can see, I patched it. Sometimes these necessary improvisations add something to a cake.

Difficult
Start two days before

INGREDIENTS

(see pp. 8 to 14 for details)
1 loaf-tin cake
2 almonds
1 to 2 packets marzipan
Bakewell paper
250g (½lb) white tragacanth icing
1 to 2 packets fondant
1 20cm (8″) square cake board
small piece of extra cake
numbers 3, 35, 1, icing tubes
food colourings, including silver

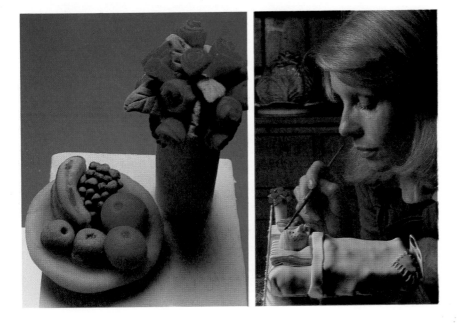

Cut away some of the top of the cake to leave the shape of a prone figure from the neck down (figs. 1, 2).

Stick two almonds in place for his feet, then cover with marzipan (figs. 3, 4).

Measure the width of the cake and, using this as a guide, draw the shapes of a bed-head and bed-end onto pieces of paper. Pin Bakewell paper over these and pipe the shapes with a no. 3 tube and white tragacanth icing, making several spares. At the same time with a no. 1 tube pipe a tiny thermometer onto the Bakewell paper (figs. 5, 6).

Make a temperature chart out of white fondant. Cover the top of the bed with a white 'undersheet' of fondant. Cover the base of the bed with the same (fig. 7).

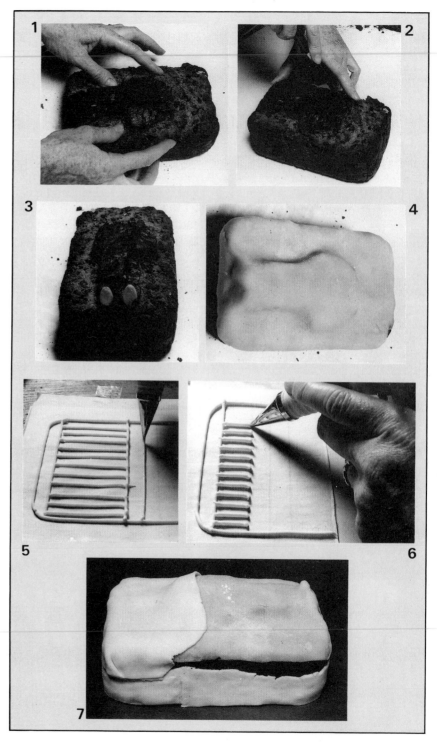

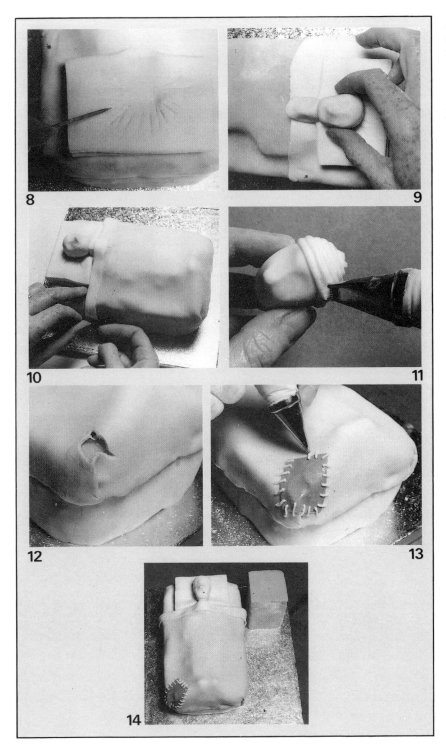

8

9

10

11

12

13

14

Make two rather thin hospital pillows out of fondant. Put in position and mark creases with a cocktail stick (fig. 8).

Colour a little fondant pale green (see p.11) and make a head and neck. Place in position (do not stick yet), (fig. 9).

Colour some fondant pale blue and cover the bed, making neat envelope corners. Fold a strip of white fondant over upper edge for top sheet, (fig. 10).

Using no. 35 tube and white royal icing pipe a bandage round the head (fig. 11). With a no. 1 tube pipe a safety pin on the side. Place head in position on pillow, sticking to neck with a little icing.

Repair any damage! (see introduction) (figs. 12, 13).

Cut extra cake into box shape. Cover with marzipan (fig. 14) and then with fondant. Make a drawer and cupboard front out of fondant. Pipe handles. Paint the temperature chart. Make miniature roses by rolling up tiny strips of red fondant. Make leaves, a vase, fruit bowl and fruit out of coloured marzipan and stick all in position. Paint features and spots on the head, and stick the thermometer in his mouth. Paint handles silver. Finally extremely carefully remove bed-ends from Bakewell paper and stick onto bed. Stick temperature chart in position.

NUDES

This cake was made for Bryan Wharton, who photographed this book, and who also happens to be a great friend of ours. It was his fortieth birthday, and as he has been known to have one or two girlfriends I thought one for each year of his life might be appropriate on his cake. It should be quite crowded if I make one for his sixtieth.

Forty little naked ladies is quite a large number to make, and this is a good opportunity to enlist the help of anyone willing. A girlfriend helped me with the modelling and my mother with painting the final details. You could always keep a lump of pink fondant in a plastic bag by the television and do a few each evening – perhaps *Miss World* or *Dallas* would be good inspiration.

Easy
Start day before

INGREDIENTS
(see pp. 8 to 14 for details)

1 20cm (8″) round cake
1 packet marzipan
1 packet fondant icing
½kg (1lb) white royal icing
numbers 8, 35, 5 and 2 tubes
food colours
non-toxic plasticine
Bakewell paper
1 25cm (10″) round cake board

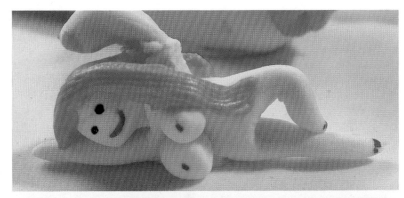

Cover the cake with marzipan (fig. 1).

Colour the fondant flesh pink (see p. 11) and make one large nude and thirty-nine small ones (or appropriate number). The large one should be propped into a sitting position to dry, and the attitudes of the small ones should be as varied as possible (figs. 2, 3). Allow to dry on Bakewell paper.

Put cake on the board. With royal icing cover smoothly the top and sides of the cake. Allow to dry. Using the no. 8 tube, pipe a shell border around the top and bottom of the cake, and with no. 5 tube pipe decorative panels around the side (figs. 4, 5).

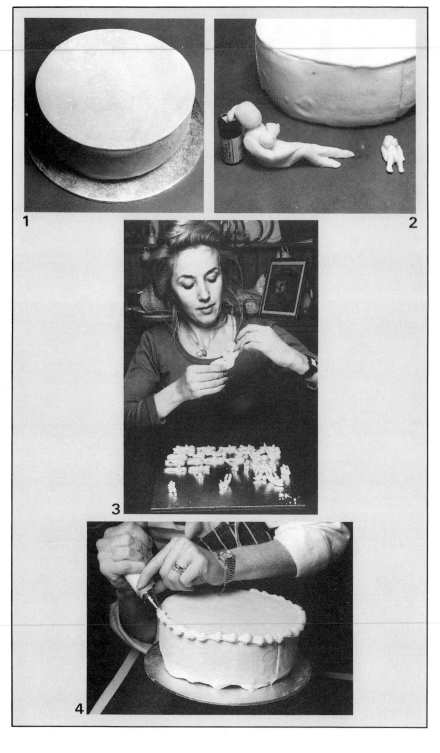

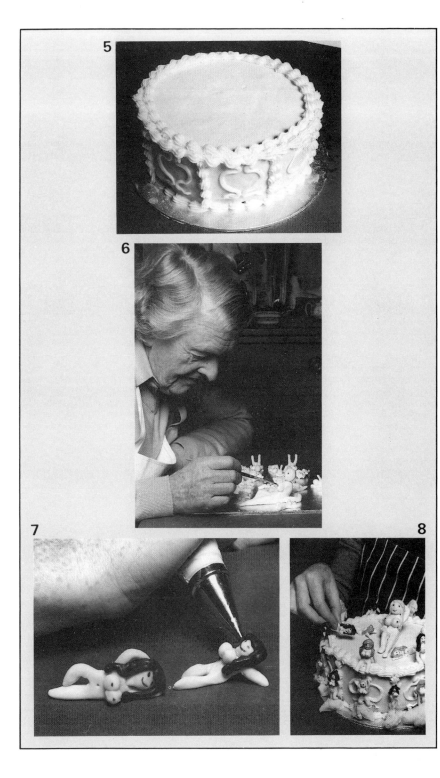

Paint on the features with a fine brush (fig. 6).

Colour small quantities of royal icing brown, yellow and red, and pipe on the hair, using a no. 2 tube for the small ladies and no. 35 for the large one (fig. 7).

Stick them in position with a little royal icing and prop them up where necessary with pieces of plasticine until dry (fig. 8).

BUNCH OF FLOWERS

A girlfriend of mine has a beautiful name – Flora. That was enough to inspire this cake, which was originally made for her birthday, as I think flowers made out of icing are always very effective. I thought that to use fondant as paper might be unusual, and would make a change from just sticking the flowers all over a traditionally shaped cake. Once I had finished it it struck me that it would also make the perfect Mother's Day cake.

The roses are really quite easy to make once you get the hang of it, and the iris – which I made by copying some real ones – are relatively simple too. Any standard cake-icing book will tell you how to make all sorts of other flowers, and it would be nice to make the bouquet match the season in which it is made.

Difficult
Start two days ahead

INGREDIENTS
(see pp. 8 to 14 for details)

1 loaf-tin cake
250g (½lb) tragacanth icing
Bakewell paper
about sixteen roses including a few
    buds
four iris flowers
1 packet marzipan
2 to 3 packets fondant
125g (¼lb) royal icing
number 2 icing tube
food colourings

Mix the tragacanth icing and colour a leafy green. With a no. 2 tube pipe several ferns onto Bakewell paper, making plenty to allow for breakages. Leave to dry for at least 24 hours (figs. 1, 2).

Shape the cake to form the centre section of the bunch (fig. 3). Cover with marzipan.

Roll out 1 packet of fondant and cut to a square. Place the cake in the middle of it and wrap the fondant up and around the cake as shown (figs. 4, 5).

Using about another ½ packet of fondant cut and place another piece across the cake to give the illusion of a further complete wrap around (fig. 6).

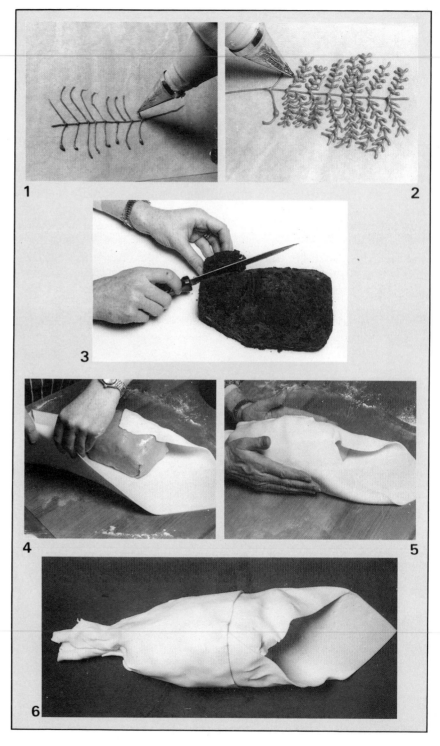

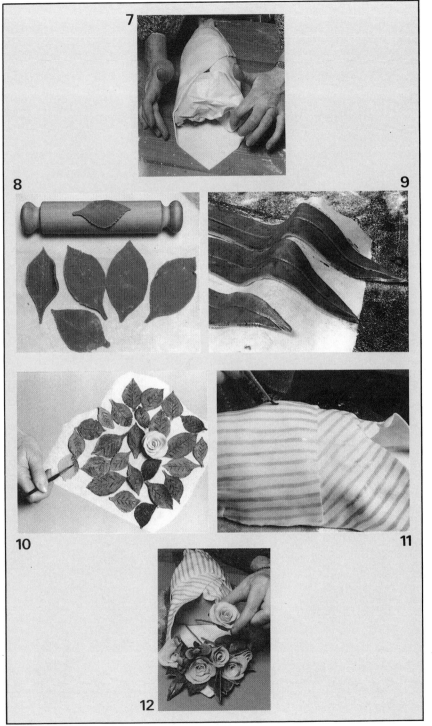

Place some crumpled paper in the opening to support the icing. Leave to dry (fig. 7).

Colour about ½ packet of fondant green and cut out some rose and iris leaves, marking veins with a knife. Dry some on crumpled paper to vary the shapes (figs. 8, 9).

Paint the leaves with dark green colouring, letting it run into the marked veins (fig. 10).

With no. 2 tube pipe a little bright yellow icing onto the iris petals. Touch up where appropriate with a little dark purple colouring. Paint pale pink stripes onto the 'paper', making sure they run the right way. Let dry a few minutes (fig. 11).

Fill with flowers and leaves, sticking them in position with royal icing and fondant where necessary (fig. 12). Remove ferns very carefully from Bakewell paper and stick one or two among the flowers.

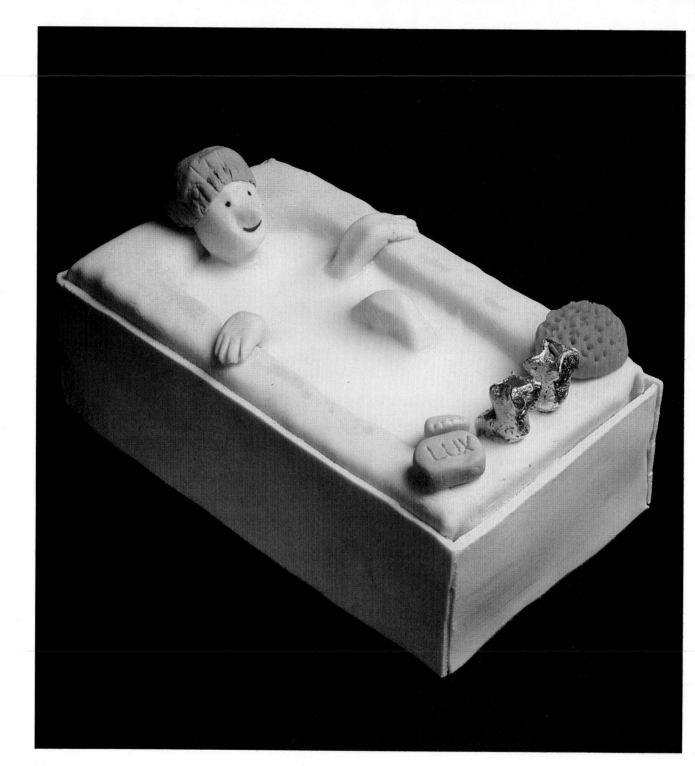

BATH

I love this lady in the bath because she looks so silly sitting in her soapy water with her hat on – quite the opposite of the glamorous models in bubble-baths with beautifully coiffured hair and full make-up that we see on television. I must confess I have been known to wear one of the dreadful bath-caps and they really don't do much for one's ego first thing in the morning.

It's very pleasing when one can bring some humour into a cake design – the tea table is hardly a place normally associated with comedy.

I made this originally for a local fête: it was to decorate a bed and bath stall and then be raffled at the end of the afternoon. It proved irresistible to investigation by various young fingers during the course of the day and the soap and sponge got well prodded. Luckily I had made some spares, as there's nothing more depressing than squashed soap on the side of the bath.

Medium difficulty
Start day before

INGREDIENTS
(see pp. 8 to 14 for details)

1 loaf-tin cake
1 packet marzipan
1 to 2 packets fondant icing
1 cocktail stick
Bakewell paper
250g (½lb) water icing
food colourings, including silver
1 25cm (10″) round cake board

Turn the cake upside-down and square off the sides neatly. Scoop out a bath shape carefully to a depth of about 15mm (¾″) with a sharp knife (figs. 1, 2, 3, 4).

Cover top and sides with marzipan. Roll out about a third of the fondant and in one piece cover the top and part of the sides, letting the fondant fit into the scooped-out centre by slitting as shown (fig. 5).

Make taps out of white fondant. Colour a little fondant flesh pink and make hands, feet, knee (not shown) and head. The hands should be shaped ready to fit over the edges of the bath. Colour a little fondant a deeper pink and make the soap. When the head has dried enough to hold its shape cover it with a blue fondant bath-cap. Make the sponge from marzipan marked with a cocktail stick. Allow all to dry on Bakewell paper (fig. 6).

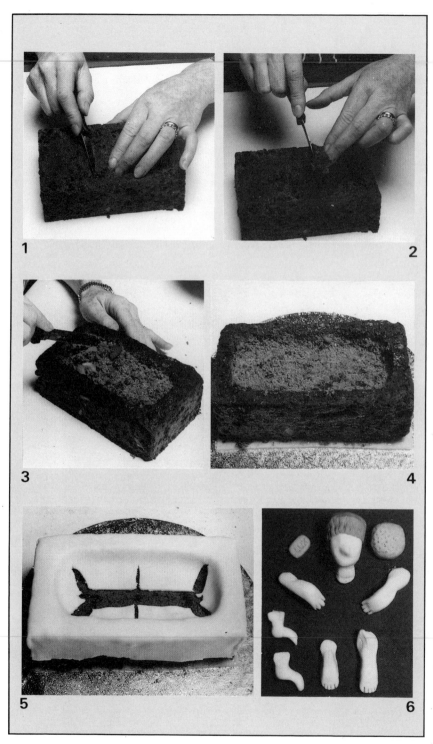

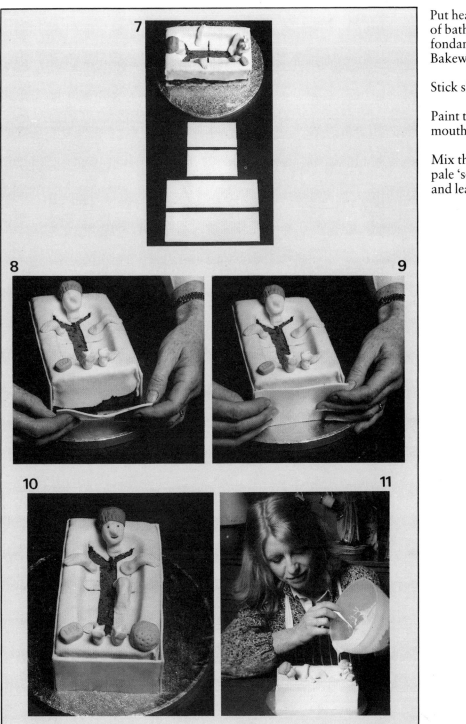

Put head etc in position. Measure sides of bath and roll and cut pieces of fondant to fit. Allow to dry slightly on Bakewell paper (fig. 7).

Stick sides to bath (figs. 8, 9).

Paint the taps silver. Paint eyes and mouth on the head (fig. 10).

Mix the water icing and colour it a very pale 'soapy' blue. Pour into the bath and leave to set (fig. 11).

CHRISTMAS SACK

It is an extraordinary British tradition that on the one day of the year when we eat what is probably our heaviest meal, we should also prepare an enormously rich cake for tea. But of course it has become as much part of Christmas fare as the turkey or the mince pies, and there would be dismay in our household if it were ever left out.

This really is an occasion to be original. If you are going to take the trouble to decorate your own Christmas cake it is worth thinking of an unusual design – the shops are full of traditional ones. The cake can make a wonderful centrepiece for the table on Christmas Day.

I thought a sack of toys would make a change. If you have children with you over Christmas then it's great fun for them to have the little parcels out of the top, and if they don't like rich fruit cake then you can easily make them by wrapping fondant around chocolate biscuits or jaffa cakes instead. To add to the 'jolly' look, Father Christmas has apparently been rather lazy in my case and left some of the presents unwrapped – or perhaps he had some trouble with one day stoppages by his gnomes.

Medium difficulty
Start two days ahead

INGREDIENTS
(see pp 8 to 14 for details)

1 20cm (8") round cake
1 packet marzipan
extra pieces of cake, or biscuits,
jaffa-cakes, etc
2 packets fondant
1 30cm (12") round cake board
250g (½lb) royal icing
number 2 icing tube
food colourings

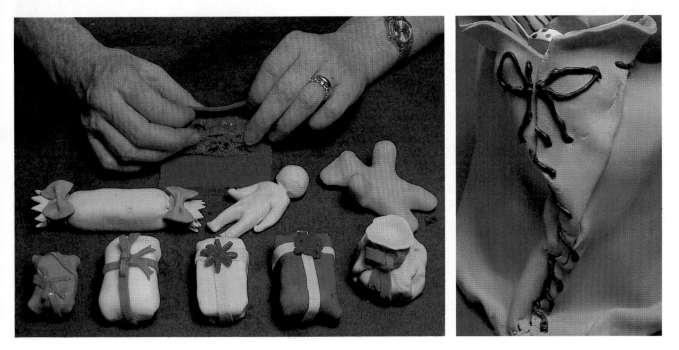

Cut two crescent shapes from sides of cake (figs. 1, 2).

Stick these with a little icing onto the top of the cake (fig. 3).

Colour some pieces of fondant in different bright colours and make some parcels by wrapping the fondant around small pieces of extra cake or biscuits etc (see introduction). Decorate with further bits of fondant and with piping. Make a doll out of pink fondant and a teddy out of marzipan (fig. 4). I also piped a tennis racquet onto Bakewell paper. Let them all dry on Bakewell paper and then decorate them further by painting with food colourings.

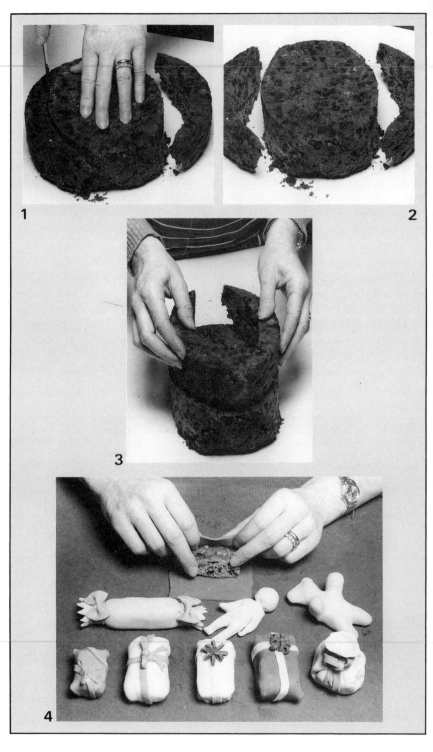

1

2

3

4

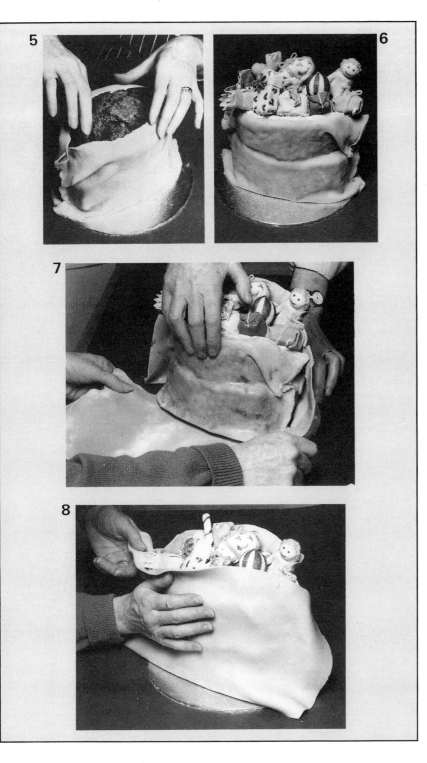

Fill the hollow of the sack with extra pieces of cake (or again biscuits etc) and cover sides roughly with marzipan (fig. 5).

Stick the toys and parcels on top with a little icing, keeping back a few (fig. 6).

Colour 1 packet of fondant brown (see p. 11) and roll out. Spread the fondant over the cake board and then, getting a friend to help, lift the cake onto the middle. Paint the sides of the cake with jam, or spread with a little icing, and quickly bring up the fondant each side into sack-like folds (figs. 7, 8). Trim each side with scissors. Let dry. Colour a little royal icing dark brown and pipe stitches onto the sides with a no. 2 tube. Position remainder of presents leaning against the sack.